CROCHET
STYLE

CROCHET STYLE

Sally Harding

WINDWARD

Crochet Style
© Frances Lincoln Limited 1987
Text © Sally Harding 1987
Garment design © Sally Harding 1987
Fashion photography © Julie Fisher 1987

Crochet Style was conceived,
edited and designed by Frances Lincoln Limited,
Apollo Works, 5 Charlton King's Road, London NW5 2SB

Windward
an imprint owned by W.H. Smith and Son Limited
Registered No. 237811, England
Trading as WHS Distributors,
St. John's House, East Street, Leicester, LE1 6NE

ISBN 0 7112 0458 6

Printed and bound in Italy
Filmsetting by Bookworm Typesetting, Manchester

CONTENTS

THE APPEAL OF CROCHET	6
STRIPES	9
BROAD STRIPES	12
STRIPED PANELS	15
CHECKED STRIPES	18
STRIPES ON STRIPES	22
STRIPES & SQUARES	26
PLAIDS & CHECKS	29
BOLD BLOCK PLAID	32
TRICOLOUR CHECK	36
TEXTURED CHECKS	38
CHECK & PLAID	41
BUFFALO PLAID	44
WOVEN PLAID	48
TEXTURES	51
CABLES	54
ZIGZAGS	57
CLUSTERS	60
BASKETWEAVE	64
MOTIFS & PATTERNS	67
FANS	72
LEAVES	76
DIAMONDS	80
COLOUR BLOCKS	83
WINTER FLOWERS	86
BOBBLED FAIR ISLE	90
WAVES & CHECKS	94
OPENWORK	97
SCALLOPED LACE	100
BOBBLED LACE	103
CHENILLE CHEQUERS	106
APPENDIX	109
CROCHET TIPS	110
TEXTURE TECHNIQUES	110
COLOUR PATTERNS	112
CROCHET EDGINGS	113
KNITTED EDGINGS	115
TUNISIAN CROCHET	116
MAKING UP	117
YARNS	118
YARN SUPPLIERS	120
ACKNOWLEDGMENTS	120

THE APPEAL OF CROCHET

The crocheted fabric offers a wealth of stitch textures, colour and yarn combinations and fashion shapes. It is therefore surprising that, during the recent expansion of knitting design, crochet has remained a poor second cousin. This book attempts to redress the balance by uncovering the versatility of crochet and taking it into the realm of fashion. Perhaps preconceptions have played a part in stifling interest in crochet. So limited is the general concept of crochet that any crochet fabric other than that of a household doily or a bright afghan is frequently met with the incredulous response — 'Is that really crochet?' To help dispel this myth and to inspire crochet enthusiasts, I have set out to illustrate some of the attractive aspects of the crocheted textile. I have used a wide range of yarns and many of the most interesting designs have resulted from effective combinations of differing yarn textures worked in simple stitches.

CROCHET YARNS

Yarn is without a doubt the most important element in crochet. Passion about the feel and look of yarns is what turns us into obsessive crocheters, knitters or weavers. So consider carefully and thoroughly the colour, texture and composition of a yarn before purchasing it.

When possible, buy natural fibres or natural fibres mixed with a small proportion of synthetic. They have a better look and feel than totally synthetic yarns. They age with grace and can withstand washing and

Cotton

Mercerised cotton yarns have a lovely sheen and produce crisp textures. They are perfect for crochet openwork and for highlights and contrasts — for instance for shiny bobbles on a wool base.

Mohair

Ideal for plaids, cables and stripes, mohair yarns are a favourite for crochet. Do not be put off by the fact that the hairs slightly obscure the crochet loops when working. It only takes a little practice to overcome this.

Chenille

Usually made of cotton, chenille sometimes has a synthetic mixture in the core to hold the short cotton fibres securely in place. Crocheted cotton chenille produces a warm and supple fabric.

Textured yarns

These include many bumpy yarns which are often called fancy or novelty yarns. The examples illustrated here are more specifically known as slub, knop and snarl yarns. Slub yarns have irregular thick and thin sections produced by looser or tighter spinning. The single strands of knop yarn are spun so that the strands double up on themselves, creating lumps intermittently. Snarl yarns have a texture rather like towelling. Little twists of yarn stick out from the core.

Metallic yarns

Evening wear is often attractively finished off by adding a glittery edging. Fine metallic yarns can also be worked together with a strand of mohair or wool for a more subtle glitter.

Wool
Smooth wool yarns have the
advantage of being available
in an extensive range of
colours. Fine tweeds are
especially effective for
crochet. When choosing wool
yarns, remember that some
100% wool yarns are softer
than others. Always check the
softness.

pressing. Unlike some synthetics, natural fibres breathe with your skin and can provide warmth, coolness and comfort.

There is a vast variety of yarns available today. The key to choosing yarns to crochet is to stick to the thinner, more lightweight yarns. This does not mean that the yarn will require a fine hook and that your garment will take weeks to make. Generally a better crochet fashion fabric is achieved by using a comparatively large hook to work the finer yarns loosely. Because of the structure of the loops, crochet creates a doubled fabric and can become stiff and unwearable when thick yarns are worked tightly. Experiment with any fine and lightweight yarns you have. Appealing crochet fabrics are also made with the fluffy or textured yarns such as mohairs, chenilles, slubs and loop yarns worked in simple double crochet, half treble or treble.

Some of the yarns most suitable for crochet are reproduced life-size on the previous pages. These are the weights which are the starting point for successful crochet fashion. On page 119 there are life-size photographs of the yarns used for the patterns in the book to help you choose a substitute yarn.

FASHION DESIGNS

The patterns in the book are divided into five distinct design categories covering stripes, plaids and checks, textures, colour stitches and motifs and openwork. Each section is introduced by a selection of stitch variations which can be used as alternatives in the patterns or as a design guide for more advanced crocheters. Many of the sweater patterns are accompanied by alternative colourways or fashion design variations. This provides a wide range of garment shapes, fabrics and colour combinations.

CROCHET TECHNIQUES

Although some of the crochet fabrics in the book may look unusual or complicated, only the simplest crochet stitches have been used. Anyone with basic crochet skills could work the designs, provided that they follow the step-by-step instructions in the last chapter for the more difficult techniques. This chapter also includes a list of crochet tips which are an invaluable guide to successful crochet. Even advanced crocheters would be wise to read these tips carefully before commencing any crochet project to ensure a good fit and a professional finish.

Sally Harding

STRIPES

STRIPES

Stripes are the simplest of all design patterns. Depending on the stripe and the colours, they can make a garment sporty, elegant or classic. Here are some samples illustrating how widely different stripes can look. They can be used as variations for the stripe patterns in the designs that follow or they may inspire the creation of original variations.

► SIMPLE STRIPES

The simplest stripe is made by introducing one or two rows of a contrasting colour into a solid background. From this elementary beginning endless combinations follow by adding to the number of colours and varying the depth of the stripes. The stripes in samples 1 and 2 are examples of simple stripes in softly contrasting colours. Worked in half treble, these stripes could easily be worked as an alternative design on *Stripes on stripes* (page 22) or *Checked stripes* (page 18).

► RANDOM STRIPES

Random stripes in double crochet (7) are a perfect way to use up leftover yarns. Yarns similar in weight should be used. It is possible to introduce textured yarn intermittently with smooth yarns provided it is introduced at random *evenly* across the piece being crocheted. If worked in only one area, it may make the crochet longer or shorter on one side. When smooth and textured yarns are being matched, the textured yarn should appear much thinner because the hairs or loops will add considerable bulk even though the threads actually look fine.

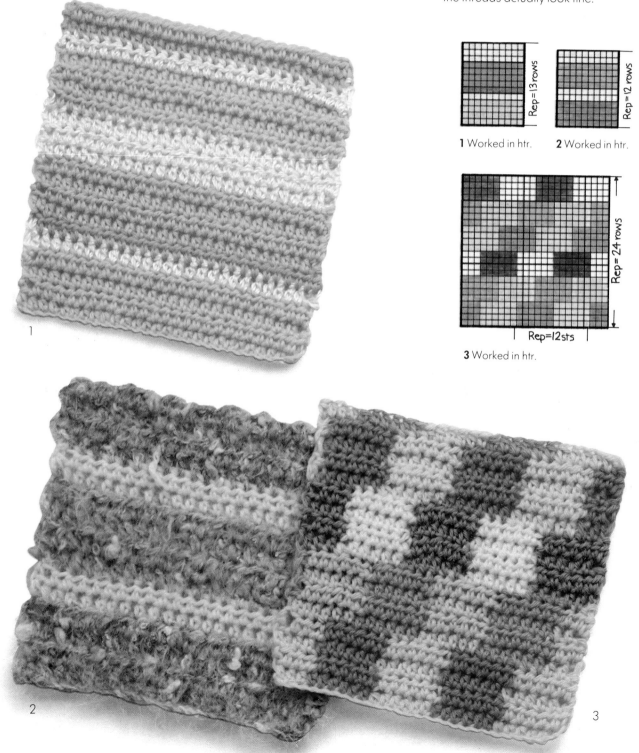

1 Worked in htr.　　2 Worked in htr.

3 Worked in htr.

1

2

3

▶ ADVANCED STRIPES

More complicated than horizontal stripes, diagonal stripes (3 and 4) use two colours in a row. If you juxtapose contrasting stripe panels you achieve an even more complicated stripe construction, but one that is still easy to work. Sample 5 would be a possible substitute for the stripes in *Stripe panels* (page 15). Irregular or wavy vertical stripes (6) soften the crisp, harder edge of straight stripes. One way of forming vertical stripes is to work the body of the garment from side seam to side seam instead of in the usual way which is from lower edge to top.

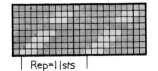

| Rep=11 sts |

4 Worked in tr.

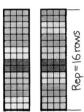

5 Tunisian crochet knit stitch.

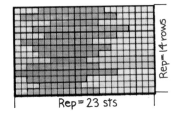

| Rep = 23 sts |

6 Worked in dc.

7 Random stripes in dc.

7

6

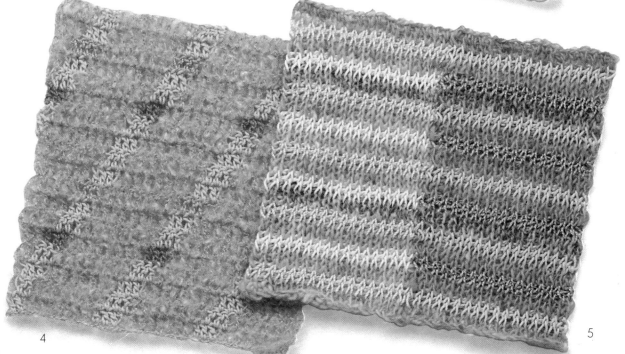

4

5

BROAD STRIPES

A mixed rayon yarn gives a subtle sheen to this classic jacket shape. The striped crochet fabric is worked in a simple pattern of double crochet and chain stitches. For a variation, create an original design with wider or narrower stripes.

▶ **SIZES**

To fit 86[91:96]cm/34[36:38]in bust.
Note: Figures for larger sizes are in square brackets. If there is only one set of figures, it applies to all sizes. *See diagram for finished measurements.*

▶ **MATERIALS**

See page 118 for further yarn information
Use a medium weight acrylic and rayon yarn (approx 117m per 50g):
600[650:700]g in main colour MC (cream)
150g in contrasting colour A (blue)
100g in contrasting colour B (white)
4.50mm crochet hook *or size to obtain correct tension*
4 buttons
Shoulder pads (optional)

▶ **TENSION**

24 sts and 23 rows to 10cm over patt st using 4.50mm hook.
Check your tension before beginning (see Note below).

Note: Back, fronts and sleeves are worked in rows which progress from side seam to side seam instead of from lower edge to top in the usual way. When counting sts, remember to count each dc and each 1ch space.

▶ **BACK**

***Using MC, make 92ch.
Base row 1dc into 2nd ch from hook, *1ch, miss next ch, 1dc into next ch, rep from * to end. Turn. 91 sts counting each ch sp and each dc as a st or 46dc.
1st row 1ch, 1dc into first dc, *1ch, 1dc into next dc, rep from * to end. Turn. Last row forms patt st and is rep throughout. Work 4[6:6] rows more in patt st.
Armhole shaping
Next row 1ch, work (1dc, 1ch, 1dc) into first dc — called 'inc 2 at beg of row' —, *1ch, 1dc into next dc, rep from * to end. Turn.
Next row 1ch, 1dc into first dc, *1ch, 1dc into next dc, rep from * to last dc, end with (1ch, 1dc) twice into last dc — called 'inc 2 at end of row'. Turn.
Rep last 2 rows twice more.*** 103 sts.
Next row 45[47:49]ch, 1dc into 2nd ch from hook, *1ch, miss next ch, 1dc into next ch, rep from * to end of ch, then

cont in patt to end of row. Turn. 147[149:151] sts.
Work 4 rows without shaping.
Drop MC at edge of work but do not break off.
Using A, work one row without shaping.
Shoulder shaping
Using A, inc 2 at beg of next row. Break off A.
Using MC, work 5 rows without shaping. Inc 2 at beg of next row.
Rep from ** to ** once more.
Using A, work 2 rows without shaping. Break off A.
Using MC, work 3 rows without shaping.
Cont in MC, inc 2 at beg of next row. Work 5[5:7] rows without shaping. 155[157:159] sts.
Neck shaping
Keeping to patt st, dec 2 sts at beg of next row (neck edge). 153[155:157]sts.
Note: Dec 2 sts at beg of a row by working 1ch, miss first dc and work first dc into next dc.
Using MC, work 2 rows without shaping.

Using A, work 2 rows. Break off A.
*Using MC, work 12 rows.
Using A, work 2 rows. Break off A.*
Rep from * to * once more. Work 3 rows in MC.
Inc 2 at neck edge on next row. 155[157:159] sts. This completes neck shaping.
Work 2nd shoulder and armhole as for first side of back, reversing shaping and working stripe patt as set. Fasten off.

▶ **LEFT FRONT**

Work as for back from *** to ***. 103 sts.
Next row 45[47:49]ch, using B, work 1dc into 2nd ch from hook, (1ch, miss next ch, 1dc into next ch) 10[11:11] times, using MC, *1ch, miss next ch,

1dc into next ch, rep from * to end of ch, then cont in patt to end of row. Turn. 147[149:151] sts.
Next row Using MC, 1ch, 1dc into first dc, *1ch, 1dc into next dc, rep from * to within last dc in MC (not *into* last dc in MC), using B, 1ch and cont in patt to end. Turn.
Next row Using B, work over all dc in B, then using MC, 1ch and cont in patt to end. Turn.
Cont in this way for 2[2:4] rows more, moving B one st further from shoulder edge in each row.
Work one row in A.
Shoulder shaping
Work shoulder shaping as for back, keeping to stripe sequence as set on back and cont to add one more st in B with each row in between stripes in A.

155[157:159] sts.
Note: To keep an even slope formed by MC and B, remember to move B over 3 sts after each stripe in A.
Neck shaping
Keeping to patt st and stripe patt as set, shape neck as foll:
Next row With RS facing miss first 16[18:20] sts (8[9:10]dc) and rejoin B to next st with a ss, 1ch, 1dc into same dc as ss was worked, work in patt to end of row. Turn.
Dec 2 sts at neck edge on next 4 rows, so ending with 2nd row of a stripe in A.
Note: Dec 2 sts at end of row by working to last 2dc of row, 1ch as usual, insert hook into next dc, yrh and draw a loop through, insert hook into last dc, yrh and draw a loop through, yrh and draw through all 3 loops on hook.
Break off MC.
Dec 2 sts at neck edge on next 2 rows

and then on every alternate row 8 times *and at the same time* work last 19 rows of left front in stripe sequence of 12 rows in B, 2 rows in A and 5 rows in B. 111 sts.

▶ RIGHT FRONT

Patt st is reversible so that right front is worked exactly as for left front to 4th stripe in A.

Work first row in A as for left front, then work buttonhole row as foll:

Buttonhole row Using A (and beg at neck edge), work first 9 sts (5dc) in patt st, *5ch, miss next 5 sts (1ch-1dc-1ch-1dc-1ch) and cont in patt st across next 26 sts, rep from * twice more, 5ch, miss next 5 sts and cont in patt to end of row. Turn.

On next row work in patt st across 5ch of each buttonhole and complete as for left front.

▶ SLEEVES (make 2)

Using MC, make 10ch and work base and first rows as for back. 9 sts.

Next row 15[13:11]ch, 1dc into 2nd ch from hook, *1ch, miss next ch, 1dc into next ch, rep from * to end of ch, then cont in patt st to end of row. Turn.
Work one row without shaping.
Rep last 2 rows 0[1:2] times more. 23[33:39] sts.

Next row 15[13:11]ch, 1dc into 2nd ch

Narrower stripes in a brighter colourway produce a more sporty jacket.

Cont in stripe sequence of 2 rows A and 12 rows MC as set on back *and at the same time* inc 2 at sleeve top on next row, work 7 rows without shaping, inc 2 at beg of next row, work 13 rows without shaping (this is centre of sleeve). 133[135:137] sts. Work 14 rows more in patt without shaping, then work 2nd side of sleeve shaping as for first side, reversing shaping. Fasten off.

▶ **POCKETS** (make 2)
Using MC, make 54[56:58]ch. Work base and first rows as for back. 53[55:57] sts *or* 27[28:29]dc.
Work 11 rows more in MC, 2 rows in A, 12 rows in MC, 2 rows in A, 13 rows in MC *and at the same time* shape side seam of pocket by inc 2 at side seam edge on every 10th row 3 times in all. 59[61:63] sts.

▶ **MAKING UP**
Do not press.
Join shoulder seams. (Sew 1cm wide fabric tape along shoulder seam for firmer seam if desired.) Set in sleeves. Join sleeve and side seams.
Sew on pockets overlapping 2.5cm onto back and sewing overlapping edge parallel to side seam so that top of pocket stands out slightly from jacket. Using matching colours and with RS facing, beg at right shoulder seam and work dc evenly along back neck, down left front, along lower edge and up right front, working 2dc into lower corners. Join with a ss to first dc and fasten off. Sew on buttons opposite buttonholes. Sew in shoulder pads if desired.

DESIGN VARIATION
▶ **ALTERNATIVE STRIPES**
For a simple striped jacket omit sections in B or create an original stripe design, using wider or narrower stripes or increasing number of colours.

from hook, *1ch, miss next ch, 1dc into next ch, rep from * to end of ch, then cont in patt st to end of row, inc 2 in last st (top of sleeve). Turn.
Cont inc 14[12:10] sts along sleeve seam on every alternate row and 2 sts at top of sleeve on every row until 13[15:17] rows have been worked from beg (including base row). 111[111:107] sts.
Next row Using A, work in patt st, inc 2 at top of sleeve. Turn. 113[113:109] sts.
Next row Using A, work in patt st inc 10[12:18] sts along sleeve seam at beg of row. Turn. 123[125:127] sts. Break off A. Then using MC and keeping lower sleeve edge straight, cont to shape sleeve top. Inc 2 at sleeve top on next row and then on every alternate row twice more. Work 7 rows without shaping.

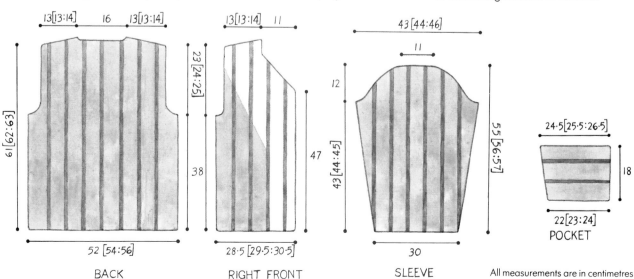

BACK RIGHT FRONT SLEEVE POCKET

All measurements are in centimetres.

STRIPED PANELS

Panels of textured tweed stripes in Tunisian crochet knit stitch have been sewn together to make this unusual sweater. The neck is finished with a roll collar and the back and front can be made with a straight lower edge as an alternative.

▶ SIZES
To fit 81-86[91-96]cm/32-34[36-38]in bust.

Note: Figures for larger size are in square brackets. If there is only one set of figures, it applies to both sizes.
See diagram for finished measurements.

▶ MATERIALS
See page 118 for further yarn information
Use a fine wool tweed yarn (approx 100m per 25g):
100[125]g in each of A (brown), F (rust-brown) and G (grey)
125[150]g in B (gold-brown)
125[175]g in D (beige)
175[200]g in C (red)
75[100]g in E (rose)
50[75]g in H (white)
5.00mm Tunisian crochet hook *or size to obtain correct tension*
3.50mm crochet hook
Shoulder pads (optional)

▶ TENSION
20 sts to 9.5cm and 25 loop rows to 10cm over Tunisian knit st using 5.00mm Tunisian crochet hook.
Check your tension before beginning.

Note: Back, front and sleeves are each made in vertical strips of Tunisian crochet which are then sewn tog. When changing colours work last yrh of return row in new colour (see page 116).

▶ BACK
Panel 1
Using A, make 20[22]ch and beg Tunisian knit st as foll:
Base row Insert hook into 2nd ch from hook, yrh and draw a loop through, *insert hook into next ch, yrh and draw a loop through, rep from * to end of ch. (Do not turn at end of rows.) 20[22] loops on hook.
1st row (return row) Yrh and draw through first loop on hook, *yrh and draw through 2 loops on hook, rep from * until there are 2 loops rem on hook, drop A at side of work but do not break off, using B, yrh and draw through last 2 loops on hook (this forms first loop of next row).
2nd row (loop row) Using B, miss first vertical loop in row below and insert hook from front to back through 2nd vertical loop (under the chain), yrh and draw a loop through, * insert hook through next vertical loop, yrh and draw a loop through, rep from * to end.
Note: To form a firm edge, insert hook through centre of last loop at the edge making sure that there are 2 vertical strands of yarn on hook at extreme left-hand edge.
3rd row Using B, as first row, changing to C with last yrh of row.
4th row Using C, as 2nd row.
5th row Using C, as first row, changing to A with last yrh of row.
6th row Using A, as 2nd row.
First-6th rows form dark stripe patt.
Rep first-6th rows 35[37] times more,

so ending with a return row in A. 109[115] loop rows worked from beg counting base row.
Break off A, B and C, but do not fasten off.
Beg with D, change to light stripe patt of one loop row in D, one in E and one in F, working return rows in matching colours as before.
Work 19 loop rows in all in lighter stripe patt as set, ending with a return row. 128[134] loop rows worked from beg counting base row. Fasten off.
Panel 2
Using G, make 20[22]ch and work base and first rows as for panel 1.
Beg with C, work in dark stripe patt of one loop row in C, one in F and one in G until 109[115] loop rows have been worked from beg counting base row, so ending with a return row in G.
Beg with H, change to light stripe patt of one loop row in H, one in D and one in E.
Work 28 loop rows in all in light stripe patt as set, ending with a return row.
Neck shaping
Keeping to light stripe patt, dec one st at beg of next 2 loop rows by missing one st at beg of row. 18[20] sts.
Work one loop row more, ending with a return row. 140[146] loop rows worked from beg counting base row. Fasten off.
Panel 3
Using A, make 20[22]ch and work base and first rows as for panel 1.
Beg with B, work in dark stripe patt as for panel 1 until 97[103] loop rows have been worked from beg counting base row, so ending with a return row in A. Beg with D, work 61 loop rows in light stripe patt as for panel 1, ending with a return row.
Neck shaping
Break off yarn and fasten off, then keeping to light stripe patt, draw up loops in last 4 sts of row and work a return row on these 4 sts. Dec one st at

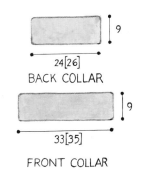

BACK COLLAR
24[26]
9

FRONT COLLAR
33[35]
9

SLEEVE
56
40
5

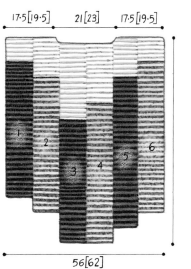

17·5[19·5] 21[23] 17·5[19·5]
56[62]
99[99]
BACK

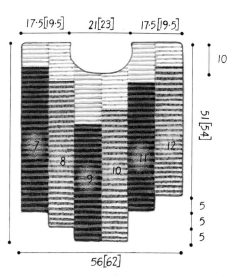

17·5[19·5] 21[23] 17·5[19·5]
10
51[54]
5
5
5
56[62]
FRONT

All measurements are in centimetres.

beg of next row and work a return row on hook. 3 sts.
Work a loop row and draw through all 3 loops on hook. 161[167] loop rows worked from beg. Fasten off.

Panel 4
Using G, make 20[22]ch and work base and first rows as for panel 1.
Beg with C, work in dark stripe patt as for panel 2 until 112[118] loop rows have been worked from beg, so ending with a return row in G.
Beg with H, work 46 loop rows in light stripe patt as for panel 2, ending with a return row.

Neck shaping
Keeping to patt, work into first 3 sts, leaving rem sts in row unworked. 4 loops on hook.
Work a return row. Dec one st at end of next row by missing 2nd to last st in row. 3 loops on hook. Work a return row and a loop row, then draw through all 3 loops on hook. 161[167] loop rows worked from beg. Fasten off.

Panel 5
Using A, make 20[22]ch and work base and first rows as for panel 1.
Beg with B, work in dark stripe patt as for panel 1 until 121[127] loop rows have been worked from beg, so ending with a return row in A.
Beg with D, work 28 loop rows in light stripe patt as for panel 1, ending with a return row.

Neck shaping
Keeping to patt, dec one st at end of next 2 loop rows. Work one loop row more, ending with a return row. 152[158] loop rows worked from beg. Fasten off.

Panel 6
Using G, make 20[22]ch and work base and first rows as for panel 1.
Beg with C, work in dark stripe patt as for panel 2 until 121[127] loop rows have been worked from beg, so ending with a return row in G.
Beg with H, work 19 loop rows in light stripe patt as for panel 2, ending with a return row. 140[146] loop rows worked from beg. Fasten off.

▶ FRONT
Panel 7
Work as for panel 6, but using dark and light stripe patts as for panel 1.

Panel 8
Using G, make 20[22]ch and work base and first rows as for panel 1.
Beg with C, work in dark stripe patt as for panel 2 until 121[127] loop rows have been worked from beg, so ending with a return row in G.
Beg with H, work 16 loop rows in light stripe patt as for panel 2, ending with a return row.

Neck shaping
Keeping to patt, dec one st at beg of next loop row. Work 4 loop rows

without shaping. Dec one st at beg of next loop row. Cont without shaping until 31 loop rows in all have been worked in light stripe patt, ending with a return row. 152[158] loop rows worked from beg. Fasten off.

Panel 9
Using A, make 20[22]ch and work base and first rows as for panel 1.
Beg with B, work in dark stripe patt as for panel 1 until 97[103] loop rows have been worked from beg, so ending with a return row in A.
Beg with D, work 42 loop rows in light stripe patt as for panel 1, ending with a return row.

Neck shaping
Break off yarn and fasten off, then keeping to stripe patt, draw up loops in last 10 sts of row and work a return row. Dec one st at beg of next 8 loop rows. Work one more loop row and draw through 2 rem loops on hook. 149[155] loop rows worked from beg. Fasten off.

Panel 10
Using G, make 20[22]ch and work base and first rows as for panel 1.
Beg with C, work in dark stripe patt as for panel 2 until 112[118] loop rows have been worked from beg, so ending with a return row in G.
Beg with H, work 27 loop rows in light stripe patt as for panel 2, ending with a return row.

Neck shaping
Keeping to patt, work next loop row until 10 loops are on hook, leaving rem sts in row unworked. Dec one st at end of next 8 loop rows. Work one more loop row and draw through 2 loops on hook. 149[155] loop rows worked from beg. Fasten off.

Panel 11
Using A, make 20[22]ch and work base and first rows as for panel 1.
Beg with B, work in dark stripe patt as for panel 1 until 109[115] loop rows have been worked from beg, so ending with a return row in H.
Beg with D, work 16 loop rows in light stripe patt as for panel 1, ending with a return row.

Neck shaping
Keeping to patt, dec one st at end of next loop row. Work 4 loop rows without shaping. Dec one st at end of next loop row. Cont without shaping until 31 loop rows have been worked in light stripe patt, ending with a return row. 140[146] loop rows worked from beg.
Fasten off.

Panel 12
Work as for panel 1, but using dark and light stripe patts as for panel 2.

▶ SLEEVES (make 2)
Panel 13
Using A, make 20ch and work base and first rows as for panel 1.

Cont in dark stripe patt beg with one loop row in C, then one in B and one in A until 51 loop rows have been worked from beg counting base row and ending with a return row.

Side shaping
Dec one st at each end of next row and then at each end of every foll 12th row 4 times more *and at the same time* work 22 loop rows more in dark stripe patt, so ending with a return row in A, then work 27 loop rows in light stripe patt beg with one loop row in D, then one in F and one in E. 10 sts. Work one loop row without shaping, ending with a return row. 101 loop rows worked from beg. Fasten off.

Panel 14
Using G, make 20ch and work base and first rows as for panel 1.
Cont in dark stripe patt beg with one loop row in F, then one in C and one in G until 51 loop rows have been worked from beg, so ending with a return row.

Side shaping
Shape sides as for panel 13 *and at the same time* work 10 loop rows more in dark stripe patt, so ending with a return row in G, then work 39 loop rows in light stripe patt beg with one loop row in H, then one in E and one in D. 101 loop rows worked from beg. Fasten off.

Panels 15 and 17
Work as for panel 13.
Panels 16 and 18
Work as for panel 14.

▶ COLLAR
Using D, make 50[54]ch for back collar. Work base and first rows as for panel 1. Work 22 loop rows, ending with a return row. Collar measures approx 9cm. Fasten off.
Using D, make 70[74]ch for front collar and work as for back collar.

▶ MAKING UP
Pin all pieces (except collar) to correct measurements face down on a padded surface. Press on WS with a warm iron and damp cloth. Sew panels tog foll diagram to form back, front and sleeves. Work seam by overlapping last st of one panel over first st of adjacent panel, lining up stripes row for row and working a running st through both layers.
Join shoulder and collar seams. Sew on collar. Mark position of sleeves 28cm from shoulder seams and sew sleeves in place between markers. Using ordinary crochet hook, work a round of dc evenly around lower edge of back and front and sleeves, using D for sleeve edge and A for body and working 2dc at outside corners and missing one st at inside corners.
Sew side and sleeve seams. Sew in shoulder pads if desired.

DESIGN VARIATION

► **PULLOVER WITH STRAIGHT LOWER EDGE**

To work a straight lower edge instead of the stepped edge inc the number of rows in dark stripe patt before beg light stripe patt as foll:

Panels 1 and 12

Work a total of 145[151] loop rows in dark stripe patt (instead of the 109[115] for stepped edge).

Panels 2 and 11

Work a total of 133[139] loop rows in dark stripe patt (instead of 109[115]).

Panels 6 and 7

Work a total of 145[151] loop rows in dark stripe patt (instead of 121[127]).

Panels 5 and 8

Work a total of 133[139] loop rows in dark stripe patt (instead of 121[127]). Work all other panels as for stepped edge pullover.

17

CHECKED STRIPES

This boldly striped mohair sweater in half trebles with crochet ribbing would look effective in many colour combinations. Leave off the collar and omit the stripes for a quick easy-to-crochet project.

SIZES

To fit 81[86-91:96-102]cm/32[34-36: 38-40]in bust.
Note: Figures for larger sizes are in square brackets. If there is only one set of figures, it applies to all sizes.
See diagram for finished measurements.

MATERIALS

See page 118 for further yarn information
Use a lightweight mohair yarn (approx 150m per 50g):
450[450:550]g in main colour MC (black)
100g in each of 2 contrasting colours A (turquoise) and B (yellow)
5.00mm crochet hook *or size to obtain correct tension*

using B, 1htr into each of next 5htr, rep from *, ending last rep with 0[2:4]htr in B. Turn.
Cont foll chart, working side shaping as shown on chart, making single incs at side edges by working 2htr into first and last sts of row until there are 98[102:106]htr.
Cont without shaping until 59th chart row has been completed.
Neck shaping
Work neck shaping for back neck as indicated. Fasten off.

Note: For neck edge work decs at end of row by leaving number of sts required for dec unworked and at beg of row by working ss over number of sts required for dec.

TENSION

15htr and 12½ rows to 10cm over colour patt using 5.00mm hook.
16dc and 20 rows to 10cm over rib using 5.00mm hook.
Check your tensions before beginning.

Note: When working broken stripes in A and B, carry yarn not in use *loosely* across back of work. Always change to new colour with last yrh of previous st (see page 112). When working from chart read even-numbered rows (WS) from left to right and odd-numbered rows (RS) from right to left.

BACK

Using MC, make 78[82:86]ch.
Base row 1htr into 3rd ch from hook, 1htr into each ch to end. Turn. 76[80:84]htr.
1st row (RS) 2ch, 1htr into each htr to end. Turn.
Last row forms htr patt and is rep throughout.
Work 0[2:4] rows more in htr.
Beg working from 2nd chart row as foll:
2nd chart row (WS) 2ch, 1htr into each of first 41[43:45]htr (changing to A with last yrh of last htr — see Note above), *using A, 1htr into each of next 5htr,

FRONT

Work as for back, foll chart and working side shaping and neck shaping for front neck as indicated.

SLEEVES (make 2)

Using MC, make 51ch.
Work base and first rows as for back. 50htr.
Inc one st at each end of next row. Work 2 rows without shaping. Inc one st at each end of next row. 54htr.
Beg working from 6th row of sleeve chart, remembering to read 6th row (WS) from left to right and inc one st at each end of 7th and every foll 3rd row until there are 76htr. Cont without shaping until sleeve measures 33cm from beg or desired sleeve length. Fasten off.

BACK RIB

Using MC, make 8ch.
Base row 1ch, 1dc into 2nd ch from hook, 1dc into each ch to end. Turn. 7dc.
1st row 1ch, working into back loop only, work 1dc into each dc to end.
Last row forms rib patt and is rep throughout.
Cont in rib patt until rib fits across lower back edge. Fasten off.

▶ FRONT RIB
Work as for back rib.

▶ CUFFS (make 2)
Using MC, make 17ch. Work base and first rows as for back rib. 16dc.
Cont in rib patt as for back rib until cuff measures 20cm.
Fasten off.

▶ COLLAR
Join shoulder seams.
Using MC, make 31ch. Work base and first rows as for back rib. 30dc.
Cont in rib patt as for back rib until collar measures 42cm and fits loosely around neck edge.
Fasten off.

▶ MAKING UP
Do not press. Darn in all loose ends. Sew ribs to back and front. Sew on cuffs gathering in fullness at lower edge of sleeve. Sew sleeves to back and front. Join side and sleeve seams. Sew half of collar seam leaving rem seam open. Sew collar to neck edge, placing collar seam approx 7cm from left shoulder seam.

DESIGN VARIATION

▶ SOLID COLOUR PULLOVER
For a simple solid colour pullover, follow instructions omitting stripes and collar.

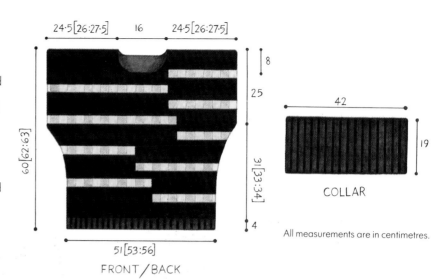

24·5[26:27·5] 16 24·5[26:27·5]

8

25

60[62:63]

31[33:34]

4

51[53:56]

FRONT/BACK

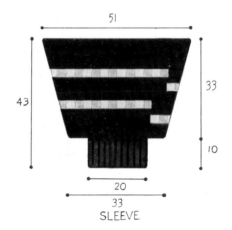

42

19

COLLAR

All measurements are in centimetres.

51

43

33

10

20

33

SLEEVE

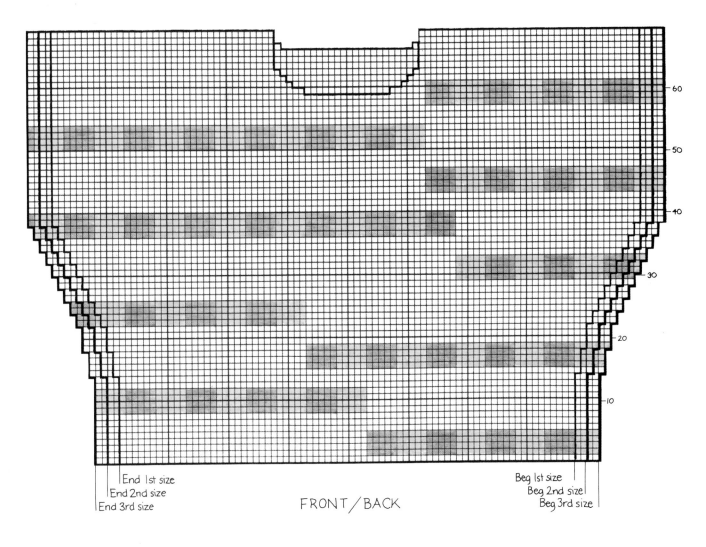

End 1st size
End 2nd size
End 3rd size

Beg 1st size
Beg 2nd size
Beg 3rd size

FRONT/BACK

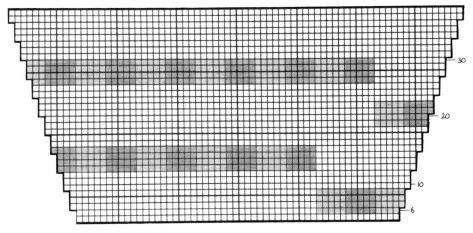

SLEEVE

21

STRIPES ON STRIPES

Contrasting stripes combine to create triangle shapes at both sides of the front and back of this loose-fitting sweater. The cuffs and neckline are bordered by a rolled edging with a crochet rib.

▶ SIZES
To fit 81[86:91:96-102]cm/ 32[34:36:38-40]in bust.
Note: Figures for larger sizes are in square brackets. If there is only one set of figures, it applies to all sizes. *See diagram for finished measurements.*

▶ MATERIALS
See page 118 for further yarn information
Use a lightweight wool yarn (approx 67m per 25g):
425[425:450:475]g in A (blue)
100[100:125:125]g in B (rust)
100g in C (pale blue)
75g in D (yellow)
5.00mm and 5.50mm crochet hooks *or size to obtain correct tension*

▶ TENSION
15htr and 13 rows to 10cm over stripe patt using 5.00mm hook.
Check your tension before beginning.

Note: When working narrow and broad stripes in the same row, do not carry yarns across the row but use a separate ball of yarn for each area of colour. When changing colours, change to new colour with last yrh of previous htr, keeping yarn on WS (see page 112). Read odd-numbered chart rows (RS) from right to left and even-numbered rows (WS) from left to right.

▶ BACK
Using smaller hook and A, make 11ch and beg rib as foll:
Base rib row 1dc into 2nd ch from hook, 1dc into each ch to end. Turn. 10dc.
1st rib row 1ch, working into *back* loops only, 1dc into each dc to end. Turn.
Rep last row to form rib patt. Cont in rib patt until 92[98:103:108] rows have been worked from beg, counting base row. Do not fasten off.

Turn rib sideways and work sts for back along rib row ends as foll:
2ch, 1htr into each of first 7[3:3:2] row ends, *miss one row end, 1htr into each of next 5 row ends, rep from * 12[14:15:16] times more, ending with miss one row end, 1htr into each of next 6[4:3:3] row ends, turn. 78[82:86:90]htr.
1st row 2ch, 1htr into each htr to end. Turn.
Foll chart for colour patt and beg with 8th[6th:4th:2nd] chart row, cont in htr as for last row until 87th chart row has been completed. Fasten off.

▶ FRONT
Work as for back until 79th[79th:78th:78th] chart row has been completed.
Neck shaping
Next row Work first 30[32:33:35]htr in patt foll chart. Turn, leaving rem sts unworked.
Next row 2ch, yrh and insert hook into first htr, yrh and draw a loop through, yrh and insert hook into next htr, yrh and draw a loop through, yrh and draw through all 5 loops on hook — called 2htr tog, work in patt to end. Turn. 29[31:32:34]htr.

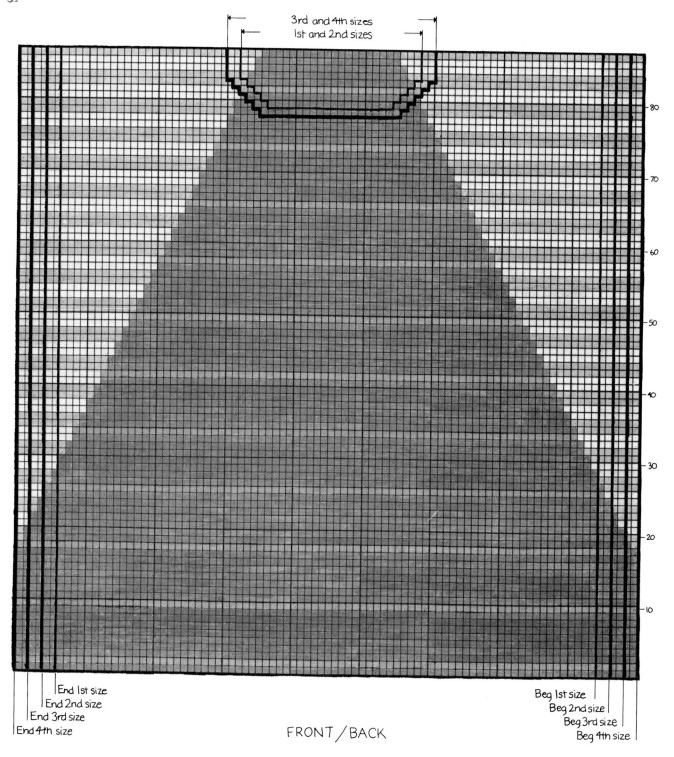

3rd and 4th sizes

1st and 2nd sizes

End 1st size
End 2nd size
End 3rd size
End 4th size

Beg 1st size
Beg 2nd size
Beg 3rd size
Beg 4th size

FRONT / BACK

Next row 2ch, work in patt to last 2htr, 2htr tog. Turn. 28[30:31:33]htr.
Cont in patt, dec one st at neck edge on next 2[2:3:3] rows. 26[28:28:30] htr.
Cont to foll chart, work last 3 rows without shaping. Fasten off.
Return to rem sts at centre front. Miss next 18[18:20:20] sts and rejoin yarn to next st, work in patt to end.
Complete to match first side, reversing shaping and foll patt from chart.

▶ **SLEEVES** (make 2)
Using smaller hook and C, make 11ch and work base and first rows as for back rib. Cont in rib patt as for back rib until 28[30:32:34] rows have been worked from beg, counting base row. Do not fasten off.
Turn rib sideways and work sts for sleeve along rib row ends as foll: 1ch, 1dc into each row end, turn. 28[30:32:34]dc.
Break off C, but do not fasten off.
Next row (WS) Using A, 2ch, working into *front* loop only of each dc, 1htr into first dc, 2htr into next dc, *1htr into next dc, 2htr into next dc, rep from * to end. Turn. 42[45:48:51]htr.

Note: Cuff edging will be worked into rem loop at top of each dc left unworked in last row.
Work one row in htr without shaping.
**Next row 2ch, 2htr into first htr, 1htr into each htr to last htr, 2htr into last htr. Turn. 44[47:50:53]htr.
Work 2 rows without shaping.**
Rep from ** to ** once more. Break off A, but do not fasten off.
Using B, work one row (WS) in htr inc one st at each end of row. 46[49:52:55]htr.
Cont in stripe sequence of 7 rows A and one row B *and at the same time* inc one st at each end of every foll 3rd row until there are 70[73:76:79]htr.
Cont in stripe patt as set without shaping until sleeve measures 46cm from beg. Fasten off.

▶ **NECKBAND**
Join shoulder seams.
Edging
Using smaller hook and B and with RS facing, work a round of dc evenly around neck edge. Then change to larger hook and work 2 rounds more,

working 1dc around stem of each st from front (see page 114). Fasten off. Edging will roll to RS.
Neck rib
Using smaller hook and C, make 7ch and work base and first rows as for back rib. Cont in rib patt as for back until neck rib, slightly stretched, fits around neck edge. Fasten off.

▶ **MAKING UP**
Do not press. Join neck rib seam. Sew neck rib to neck edge behind rolled edging. Mark positions of sleeves 23[24:25:26]cm from shoulder seams. Sew on sleeves between markers. Join side and sleeve seams.
Cuff edging
Using larger hook and B and with RS facing, hold sleeve so that cuff is uppermost and work a round of dc into rem loop at top of each dc left unworked in row above cuff rib. Then work 2 rounds more, working 1dc around stem of each st from front as for neck edging. Fasten off.
Press seams on WS with a warm iron, omitting rib.

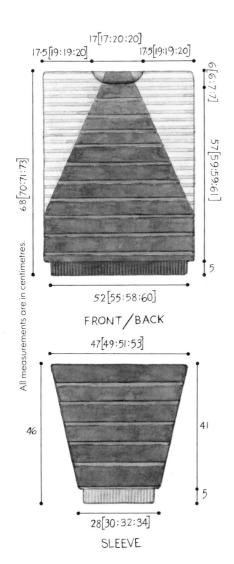

17[17:20:20]
17·5[19:19:20]   17·5[19:19:20]
6[6:7:7]
57[59:59:61]
68[70:71:73]
All measurements are in centimetres.
5
52[55:58:60]
FRONT / BACK

47[49:51:53]
46   41
5
28[30:32:34]
SLEEVE

STRIPES & SQUARES

Metallic yarn sparkles in this glittery evening top which is made in double crochet with a deep knitted ribbing. You can transform this versatile design into summer daywear by working the metallic contrasting colours in cotton yarn.

▶ SIZES

To fit 81[86:91]cm/32[34:36]in bust.
Note: Figures for larger sizes are in square brackets. If there is only one set of figures, it applies to all sizes.

The back of this evening top crosses over at the waist to give a flattering low backline.

See diagram for finished measurements.

▶ MATERIALS

See page 118 for further yarn information
Use a lightweight cotton yarn (approx 185m per 50g) and a lightweight metallic yarn (approx 160m per 20g): 140[160:185]g lightweight cotton yarn in main colour MC (black)
20g lightweight metallic yarn in each of 3 colours A (turquoise), B (rose) and C (blue)
Small amount lightweight cotton yarn in D (pink)
3.00mm and 3.50mm crochet hooks *or size to obtain correct tension*
3¾mm circular knitting needle 60cm long
Snap fasteners

▶ TENSION

23dc and 28 rows slightly stretched to 10cm over rib patt using 3.50mm hook. *Check your tension before beginning.*

Note: Crochet rib is elastic, so width of triangle on measurement diagram is approximate and is measured over only slightly stretched rib. When working with more than one colour in a row, carry yarn not in use loosely across back of work, but use separate lengths of yarn for A and D for each square. When changing colours, change to new colour with last yrh of last dc (see page 112). When working from chart, read even-numbered rows (WS) from left to right and odd-numbered rows (RS) from right to left.

▶ BODY TRIANGLE

Using larger hook and MC, make 2ch.
Base row 1dc into 2nd ch from hook. Turn. 1dc.
1st row (RS) 1ch, working into *back* loops only, work 2dc into first dc. Turn. 2dc.
Cont working into *back* loops only throughout to form crochet rib patt.
2nd row 1ch, 1dc into each dc. Turn.
3rd row 1ch, 1dc into first dc, 2dc into next dc. Turn. 3dc.
4th row 1ch, 2dc into first dc, 1dc into each dc to end. Turn. 4dc.
5th row 1ch, 1dc into each dc. Turn.
6th row As 4th row. 5dc.
7th row As 5th row.
8th row As 4th row. 6dc.
9th row 1ch, 1dc into each dc to last dc, 2dc into last dc. Turn. 7dc.
10th row As 5th row.
11th row As 9th row. 8dc.
12th row As 5th row.
13th row As 9th row. 9dc.
14th-16th rows Rep 4th-6th rows. 11dc.
Set position of square motif on next row as foll:
17th row (RS) 1ch, 1dc into first dc, changing to A with last yrh of st, using A, work 1dc into each of next 4dc, changing to MC with last yrh of last dc, using MC, 1dc into each dc to end. Turn.
18th row Work as for 4th row, but working all sts in MC in MC and all sts in A in A. Turn. 12dc. Drop MC at side of work, but do not break off.
19th row Work as for 9th row, but working all sts in MC in B and working (1dc in A, 1dc in D, 1dc in A) over 4 sts in A. Turn. 13dc.

Cont in rib patt and beg with 20th row of chart 1, foll chart for squares and stripes and for shaping.

When 116th[118th:120th] row of chart 1 has been completed (71[72:74]dc), foll chart 2 beg with 117th[119th:121st] row and working decs as indicated.

Note: For a dec at beg of row work 1ch, insert hook into first dc, yrh and draw a loop through, insert hook into next dc, yrh and draw a loop through, yrh and draw through all 3 loops on hook — called 2dc tog. For a dec at end of row, work 2dc tog over last 2 sts.

When 234th[237th:241st] row of chart has been completed (1dc), fasten off.

▶ **STRAPS** (make 2)
Using smaller hook and MC, make 2ch and beg working strap in dc (not in rib as for body) as foll:

Base row 1dc into 2nd ch from hook. Turn. 1dc.

1st row 1ch, 2dc into first dc. Turn. Drop MC, but do not break off.

2nd row Using C, 1ch, 1dc into first dc, 2dc into last dc. Turn.

3rd row Using C, 1ch, 2dc into first dc, 1dc into each dc to end. Turn. Drop C, but do not break off.

4th row Using MC, 1ch, 1dc into each

dc to last dc, 2dc into last dc. Turn.

5th row Using MC, as 3rd row.
Rep last 2 rows twice more, working 2 rows C, then 2 rows MC. 10dc.
Cont in dc without shaping, working in stripe patt of 2 rows C and 2 rows MC until strap fits along one sloped edge of body triangle. Mark last row. Cont in patt until strap measures 22cm from marker. Fasten off.

Edging
Using smaller hook and C and beg at foundation ch end of strap, work 1dc into each row end along *longer* side edge of strap. Fasten off. Using smaller hook and C and beg at same end of strap as last row, work 1ss *loosely* into each dc to end, inserting hook under both loops at top of each dc. Fasten off.

▶ **MAKING UP**
Do not press. Darn in all loose ends.

Sew straps to sloped sides of body triangle so that shaped end is at lower edge. Overlap body triangle to fit as required and pin tog.

Knitted rib
Using circular knitting needle and MC, pick up 223[237:251] evenly around lower edge of body, working through both layers where triangle overlaps (see page 115). Do not work in rounds, but work back and forth in rows of K1, P1 rib until rib measures 11.5cm. Using C, cast off loosely in rib.
Join rib seam. Adjust strap ends if necessary, adding or subtracting rows, so that straps meet at centre back neck.
Using smaller hook and C, work 1dc into each row end along other side of strap from centre front to end of strap. Sew on snap fasteners at ends of strap.

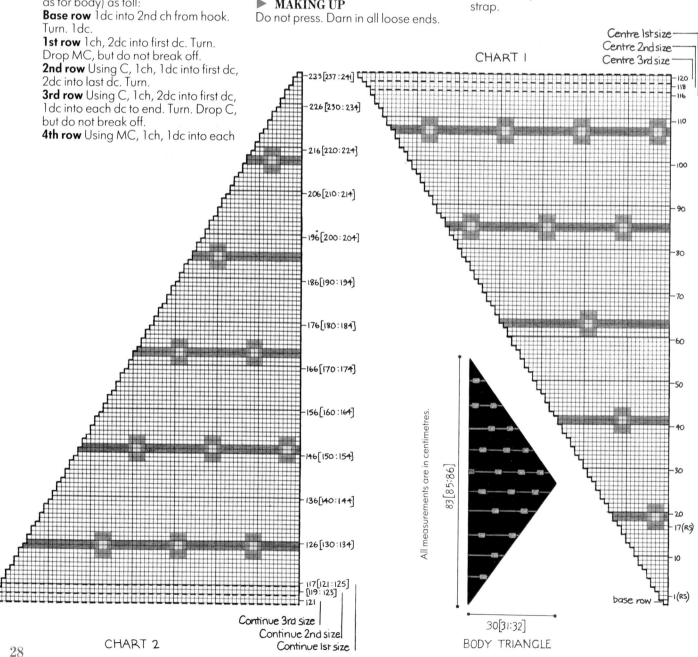

CHART 2

CHART 1

BODY TRIANGLE

Continue 3rd size
Continue 2nd size
Continue 1st size

Centre 1st size
Centre 2nd size
Centre 3rd size

All measurements are in centimetres.

83[85:86]

30[31:32]

28

PLAIDS & CHECKS

PLAIDS & CHECKS

These samples offer simple and complicated alternatives for the plaid and check garments that follow.

▶ WINDOWPANE CHECKS

The way to understand any colour design is to break it down into its basic components starting with the most elementary. For plaids or checks this would be what is called a *windowpane check*. The simple components of the windowpane check are the horizontal stripes placed at equal intervals on a solid background and crossed by regularly placed thin vertical lines. Variations are created by changing the intervals between the horizontal and vertical stripes (3).

▶ BASIC PLAIDS

Plaids begin as simple multicoloured stripes. The easiest method of transforming a striped crochet fabric into a plaid is to apply the vertical

stripes onto the completed crochet pieces. Embroidery techniques such as backstitch (3) or surface slip stitch (1 and 2) are suitable for the vertical stripes. Sample 2 is a possible alternative plaid for *Check and plaid* (page 41). The checks could be worked in colours to match the plaid.

▶ CHEQUERED PLAIDS

More complicated plaids are made by check shapes which are crossed both horizontally and vertically by thin stripes. The more variance in check shapes and the more colours, the more complex the pattern. Samples 4, 5 and 7 are examples of this type of plaid. In sample 5 the vertical stripes are worked with separate lengths of yarn

so that only 2 colours are carried across the rows (see page 112). Note how stripes of darker toned checks alternate with lighter toned checks as part of the plaid composition. In all these examples, only simple stitch techniques are used. For alternative plaids for *Bold block plaid* (page 32) and *Buffalo plaid* (page 44), try samples 4 or 5.

▶ WOVEN PLAIDS

Woven plaid (6) is a combination of crochet and weaving techniques. The base is horizontal stripes of filet crochet. The completed filet is woven vertically with strands of contrasting and matching colours.

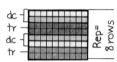

1 Vertical stripes worked in surface ss.

2 Tunisian crochet knit stitch with vertical stripes in surface ss.

3 Horizontal stripes in dc and vertical stripes in backstitch.

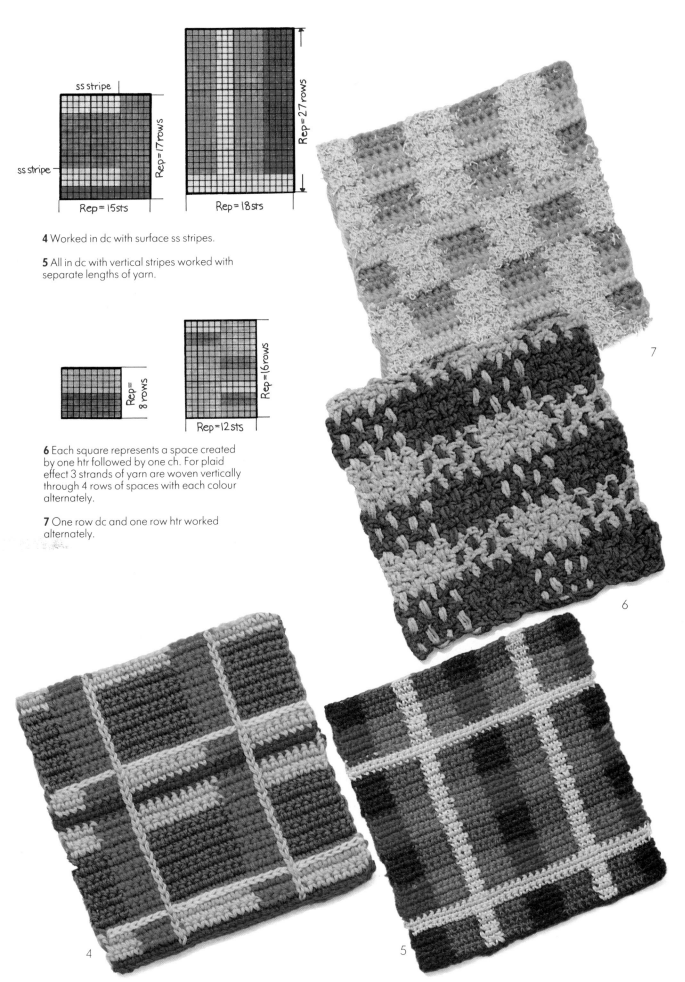

ss stripe

ss stripe

Rep = 17 rows

Rep = 15 sts

Rep = 27 rows

Rep = 18 sts

4 Worked in dc with surface ss stripes.

5 All in dc with vertical stripes worked with separate lengths of yarn.

Rep = 8 rows

Rep = 16 rows

Rep = 12 sts

6 Each square represents a space created by one htr followed by one ch. For plaid effect 3 strands of yarn are woven vertically through 4 rows of spaces with each colour alternately.

7 One row dc and one row htr worked alternately.

7

6

4

5

BOLD BLOCK PLAID

This comfortable mohair jacket with inset side pockets is crocheted in a bold plaid design. The jacket is worked in double crochet and a crisp knitted ribbing forms the collar, cuffs and mock front pocket flaps.

▶ SIZES

To fit 81[86-91:96-102]cm/32[34-36:38-40]in bust.
Note: Figures for larger sizes are in square brackets. If there is only one set of figures, it applies to all sizes.
See diagram for finished measurements.

▶ MATERIALS

See page 118 for further yarn information
Use a lightweight mohair (approx 155m per 50g) and a lightweight wool yarn (approx 120m per 50g):

250[300:350]g lightweight mohair in A (sea green)
150[150:200]g lightweight mohair in B (dark sea green)
100[100:150]g lightweight mohair in C (beige)
Small amount of a lightweight mohair in each of D (light blue), E (light green) and F (white)
150g lightweight wool yarn in G (sea green)
5.50mm crochet hook *or size to obtain correct tension*
One pair of 4mm knitting needles *or size to obtain correct tension*
7 toggle buttons
Shoulder pads (optional)

▶ TENSION

13dc and 15 rows to 10cm over block plaid patt using 5.50mm hook.
37 sts and 34 rows to 10cm over rib patt, using 4mm knitting needles.

Check your tensions before beginning.

Note: When working block plaid patt with 2 colours in a row, carry yarn not in use across top of previous row, working all sts over it. Always change to new colour with last yrh of previous st (see page 112).

▶ BACK

Using hook and A, make 66[70:72]ch loosely. Beg hem as foll:
Base row 1dc into 2nd ch from hook, 1dc into each ch to end. Turn. 65[69:71]dc.
1st row 1ch, 1dc into each dc to end. Turn.
Rep last row 2 times more to complete hem.
Beg block plaid patt as foll:
1st patt row (RS) Working into *back* loop only of each dc to form turning ridge for hem and using B, 1ch, 1dc into each of first 5[7:7]dc (changing to A with last yrh of last dc — see Note above), using A, 1dc into each of next 11[11:12]dc, using B, 1dc into each of next 11dc, using A, 1dc into each of next 11dc, using B, 1dc into each of next 11dc, using A, 1dc into each of next 11[11:12]dc, using B, 1dc into each of last 5[7:7]dc. Turn.
Last row sets position of blocks. Rep last row 3 times more, but working into *both* loops of dc of previous row throughout.
5th row Turn hem to WS along loops left unworked in 4th row and work blocks as set, working each dc into dc of previous row and into corresponding foundation ch, thus securing hem in position. Turn.
Work 6 rows more in block plaid patt as set.

12th row Work in patt as set, inc one st at each end of row by working 2dc in first and last dc, using B. Turn. 67[71:73]dc.
Work 3 rows more in block plaid patt as set. Break off B.
16th row Working in dc and beg with A, 1ch, 6[8:8]dc in A, 11[11:12]dc in C, 11dc in A, 11dc in C, 11dc in A, 11[11:12]dc in C, 6[8:8]dc in A. Turn.
Rep last row 7 times more.
24th row Work in patt as set, inc one st at each end of row. Turn. 69[73:75]dc.
Work 2 rows more in block plaid patt as set. Break off C.
27th row Working in dc and beg with B, 1ch, 7[9:9]dc in B, 11[11:12]dc in A, 11dc in B, 11dc in A, 11dc in B, 11[11:12]dc in A, 7[9:9]dc in B. Turn.
Rep last row 8 times more.
36th row Work in patt as set, inc one st at each end of row. Turn. 71[75:77]dc.
Work 5 rows more in block plaid patt as set. Break off C.
42nd row Work as for 16th row, but beg and ending with 8[10:10]dc in A. Turn.
Rep last row 10 times more.
Fasten off.

Armhole shaping
53rd row With RS facing, miss first 3[4:4]dc, join B to next dc with a ss, 1ch, 1dc into same place as ss, cont in dc across row, work all dc in A in previous row in B, and all dc in C in previous row in A, ending at last 3[4:4]dc. Turn, leaving rem dc unworked. 65[67:69]dc.
Cont in patt as set, dec one st (2dc tog) at each end of next 2 rows, then dec one st at each end of every other row 4 times. 53[55:57]dc.
Note: To work 2dc tog (insert hook into next dc, yrh and draw a loop through) twice, yrh and draw through all 3 loops on hook.
Work in block plaid patt as set without shaping until 15 rows have been completed from beg of armhole shaping. Break off A and B.
68th row (WS) Working in dc and beg with C, 1ch, 10[11:12]dc in C, 11dc in D, 11dc in C, 11dc in D, 10[11:12]dc in C. Turn.
Rep last row 10 times more. Break off D.
79th row (RS) Working in dc and beg with E, 1ch, 10[11:12]dc in E, 11dc in C, 11dc in E, 11dc in C, 10[11:12]dc in E. Turn.
Rep last row 6[8:11] times more.
Fasten off.

Shoulder and neck shaping
Keeping to block plaid patt as set in 79th row, miss first 4dc and rejoin E to next dc with a ss, 1ch and work in patt to last 4dc. Turn, leaving rem sts unworked. 45[47:49]dc.
Fasten off.
Next row Miss first 4dc and rejoin E to next dc, 1ch and work in patt across

9[9:10]dc (including dc where E is joined). Turn, leaving rem 32[34:35]dc unworked. Break off E.

Next row Using C, 1ch, work first 2dc tog, 1dc in each of next 3[3:4]dc. Fasten off.

Work 2nd side of neck as for first side, reversing shaping.

▶ LEFT FRONT

Using hook and A, make 37[39:40]ch. Work hem as for back. 36[38:39]dc. Beg block plaid patt as foll:

1st patt row (RS) Working into back loop only of each dc to form turning ridge and using A, 1ch, 1dc in each of first 5[7:7]dc, using B, 1dc into each of next 11[11:12]dc, using A, 1dc into each of next 11dc, using B, 1dc into each of last 9dc. Turn.

Last row sets position of blocks. Work 3 rows more in patt as set, working into both loops of dc of previous row throughout.

5th row Work as for 5th row of back. Work 6 rows more in block plaid patt as set.

12th row Work in patt as set, inc one st at end of row (side edge) by working 2dc into last dc. Turn. 37[39:40]dc. Cont in block plaid patt as set on back by working 15 rows of blocks in A and B, foll by 11 rows of blocks in A and C, inc one st at side edge on every 12th row twice more. 39[41:42]dc.

Work in block plaid patt without shaping until front has same number of rows to armhole shaping as back. Fasten off.

Armhole shaping

53rd row With RS facing, miss first 3[4:4]dc, join A to next dc with a ss, 1ch, 1dc into same place as ss, cont in dc across row, work all dc in C in previous row in A and all dc in A in previous row in B. Turn. 36[37:38]dc.

Cont in patt as set, dec one st at armhole edge of next 2 rows, then dec one st at armhole edge on every other

row 4 times. 30[31:32]dc.

Work in block plaid patt as set without shaping until 15 rows have been completed from beg of armhole shaping. Break off A and B.

68th row (WS) Working in dc and beg with D, 1ch, 9dc in D, 11dc in C, 10[11:12]dc in D. Turn.

Cont in block plaid patt as set in last row, work 10 rows more.

2nd and 3rd sizes only:

79th row (RS) Working in dc and beg with C, 1ch, [11:12]dc in C, 11dc in E, 9dc in C. Turn.

Cont in block plaid patt as set in last row, work [1:2] rows more.

Neck shaping

1st and 2nd sizes only:

Next row (RS) Working in dc and beg with C, 1ch, 10[11]dc in C, 11[10]dc in E. Turn, leaving rem 9[10]dc unworked. 21dc.

Fasten off.

Next row (WS) Working in block plaid patt as set, miss first 2dc and rejoin E to next dc, work to end of row. Turn. 19dc.

3rd size only:

Next row (WS) Working in block plaid patt as set, miss first 10dc and rejoin E to next dc, work to end of row. Turn. 22dc.

Next row Work in block plaid patt to last 2dc. Turn. 20dc.

All sizes:

Cont in block plaid patt, dec one st at neck edge on next 3 rows. 16[16:17]dc.

Work in block plaid patt without shaping until there are same number of rows to shoulder as for back. Keeping to patt, dec 4 sts at armhole edge on next 3 rows. 4[4:5]dc. Fasten off.

Mark positions at centre front for buttons, the first approx 1cm below neck edge, the last on 5th row from turning ridge and the other 3 evenly spaced in between.

▶ RIGHT FRONT

Work as for left front, reversing shaping and working buttonholes to match positions of buttons. Work buttonholes 3 sts in from centre front by missing 2 sts and working 2ch. On row foll buttonhole row, work 2dc into 2ch sp, catching up 2nd colour which was carried across top of previous row in order to cover this loose strand.

▶ SLEEVES (make 2)

Using hook and A, make 42[44:46]ch. Work hem as for back. 41[43:45]dc. Beg block plaid patt as foll:

1st patt row (RS) Working into back loop only of each dc to form turning ridge and using B, 1ch, 1dc into each of first 4[5:6]dc, using A, 1dc into each of next 11dc, using B, 1dc into each of next 11dc, using A, 1dc into each of last 4[5:6]dc. Turn.

Last row sets position of blocks.

Rep last row 3 times more, but working into both loops of dc of previous row throughout.

5th row Work as for 5th row of back. Keeping to block plaid patt as set in first row, inc one st at each end of next row, then at each end of foll 5th row. Cont to shape sleeve by inc one st at each end of every 6th and 5th rows alternately 3 times more, working increased sts in same colour as first and last blocks, *and at the same time*

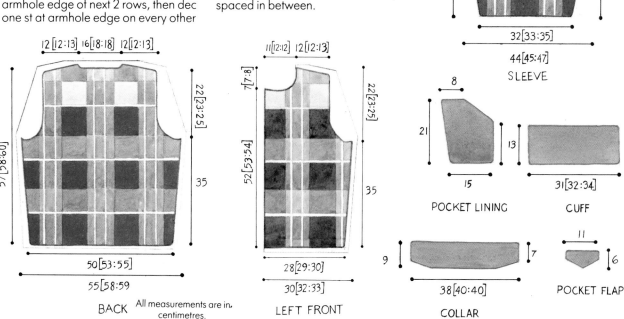

19[19:21]
11[13:15]
31[32:33]
42[45:48]
32[33:35]
44[45:47]
SLEEVE

12[12:13] 16[18:18] 12[12:13]
22[23:25]
57[58:60]
35
50[53:55]
55[58:59]
BACK All measurements are in centimetres.

11[12:12] 12[12:13]
7[7:8]
22[23:25]
52[53:54]
35
28[29:30]
30[32:33]
LEFT FRONT

8
21
13
15
POCKET LINING

31[32:34]
CUFF

9
38[40:40]
COLLAR

11
6
POCKET FLAP

work in block plaid patt of 13[15:17] rows in blocks of A and B as set in first patt row (counted from first patt row), *11 rows in blocks of A and C, 15 rows in blocks of A and B, rep block plaid sequence from * to end of sleeve. 57[59:61]dc.
Cont in block plaid patt as set without shaping until 46[48:50] rows have been worked from turning ridge. Fasten off.

Sleeve top shaping
Next row Keeping to block plaid patt as set, miss first 3[4:4]dc and rejoin yarn to next dc with a ss, 1ch, 1dc in same place as ss, work to last 3[4:4]dc. Turn.
Cont in patt, dec one st at each end of 2nd row once, at each end of every 2nd[3rd:4th] row 3 times, at each end of every row 5 times. Dec 2 sts at each end of every row twice. 25[25:27]dc. Fasten off.

▶ NECK AND FRONT EDGING
Using hook and with RS facing, beg at lower edge of left front and work a row of dc evenly up left front, around neck and down right front, using colours to match blocks being edged. Fasten off.
Using hook and C and with RS facing, beg at neck edge on left front and work a row of ss around neck, easing back neck into correct width. Fasten off.

▶ SURFACE CROCHET STRIPES
Mark the positions of horizontal surface crochet stripes on back, fronts and sleeves, the first between the first 2 horizontal rows of blocks from lower edge and the foll horizontal stripes after every 2 rows of horizontal blocks.
Mark the positions of the 2 vertical surface crochet stripes to run up the centre of each vertical row of blocks in A and C with 6dc between the 2 stripes.
Working the horizontal stripes first, work the surface crochet stripes as foll:
Using hook and F and with RS facing, insert hook from front to back through edge st and, holding yarn at back of work throughout, yrh and draw a loop through, *keeping loop on hook, insert hook through sp between next 2 sts, yrh and draw a loop through sp and through loop on hook, rep from * to end. Fasten off.
Work horizontal and vertical surface crochet stripes in the same way, inserting hook between sts for horizontal stripes and between rows for vertical stripes and working surface crochet loosely in order to avoid pulling pieces out of shape.

▶ POCKET LININGS (make 2)
Using hook and A, make 21ch. Work base and first rows as for back hem. 20dc.

Work 4 rows more in dc.
Inc one st at end of next row.
Work 11 rows more without shaping.
Inc one st at end of next row. 22dc.
Dec one st at end of next row, then dec one st at beg of next row. Rep last 2 rows until 10 sts rem.
Fasten off.

▶ CUFFS (make 2)
Using knitting needles and G, cast on 115[119:125] sts and beg rib as foll:
1st row P1, *K1, P1, rep from * to end.
2nd row K1, *P1, K1, rep from * to end.
Rep last 2 rows until cuff measures 13cm from beg.
Cast off loosely in rib.

▶ MOCK POCKET FLAPS
Using knitting needles and G, cast on 39 sts and beg rib as foll:
1st row K1, *P1, K1, rep from * to end.
2nd row Sl 1, *K1, P1, rep from * to end.
3rd row Sl 1, *P1, K1, rep from * to end.
Rep last 2 rows until flap measures 1.5cm from beg.
Next row Sl 1, rib to last 2 sts, turn leaving last 2 sts unworked.
Next row Rib to last 2 sts, turn leaving last 2 sts unworked.
Next row Rib to last 4 sts, turn leaving last 4 sts unworked.
Cont in this way, leaving 2 more sts unworked at end of each row until there are 3 sts at centre, then turn, rib 2, turn, rib 1.
Break off yarn.
Sl all sts onto one needle and cast off loosely in rib.

▶ COLLAR
Using knitting needles and G, cast on 143[149:149] sts and beg rib as foll:

1st row K1, *P1, K1, rep from * to end.
2nd row Sl 1, rib to last 45 sts, turn leaving rem sts unworked.
3rd row Rib to last 45 sts, turn leaving rem sts unworked.
4th row Rib to last 16 sts, turn leaving rem sts unworked.
5th row As 4th row.
6th row Rib to end.
7th row Sl 1, rib to end. 143[149:149] sts.
Rep last row 23 times more.
Cast off tightly in knit.

▶ MAKING UP
Do not press. Darn in all loose ends. Sew shoulder seams. Sew side seams leaving 14cm open 10cm above lower edge. Sew pocket linings into opening with straight edge along back side seam and sewing shaped edge neatly to front on WS. Sew sleeve seams and set in sleeves. Press seams lightly on WS with warm iron.
Using hook, work a row of dc evenly around pocket opening, using colours to match blocks being edged.
Mark positions of mock pocket flaps 4cm from armhole edge and then 13cm from first marker just below 3rd horizontal surface crochet stripe from lower edge. Sew flap in place between markers along top edge and short sides.
Sew collar in place 3cm from centre fronts. Sew cuff seams. Sew cast-on edge of cuff to foundation row of sleeve (beg of sleeve) inside sleeve and fold cuff to outside of sleeve.
Sew on buttons opposite buttonholes. Sew one button to each pocket flap.
If desired, sew in shoulder pads and sew small snap fastener to corner of left front at neck edge.

TRICOLOUR CHECK

Only one colour is used in each row of this easy-to-make treble crochet top. If you substitute a glitter yarn for one of the three contrasting colours, this top would be perfect for evening wear.

▶ **SIZES**
To fit 81[86:91:96-102]cm/ 32[34:36:38- 40]in bust.
Note: Figures for larger sizes are in square brackets. If there is only one set of figures, it applies to all sizes. *See diagram for finished measurements.*

▶ **MATERIALS**
See page 118 for further yarn information
Use a lightweight cotton yarn (approx 185m per 50g):
120[140:160:180]g in each of 3 colours A (blue), B (apricot) and C (cerise)
3.50mm crochet hook *or size to obtain correct tension*

▶ TENSION

26 sts and 19 rows to 10cm over check patt using 3.50mm hook.
Check your tension before beginning.

Note: When counting sts, count turning ch at beg of row as one st. To check tension make 40ch using A and work base-2nd rows of back. Cont in patt for 12cm.

▶ BACK

Using A, make 130[136:142:148]ch.
Base row 1tr into 4th ch from hook, 1tr into each of next 2ch, 3ch, miss next 3ch, *1tr into each of next 3ch, 3ch, miss next 3ch, rep from *, ending with 1tr into last ch. Turn. 128[134:140:146] sts, counting 3ch at beg of row as one st (see Note above). Drop A at edge of work, but do not break off.
1st row Using B, 3ch, 1tr into each of first 3ch missed in last row, 3ch, miss next 3tr, *1tr into each of next 3ch missed in last row, 3ch, miss next 3tr, rep from *, ending with 1dc under 3ch at end of row. Turn. Drop B at edge of work, but do not break off.
2nd row Using C, 3ch, 1tr into each of first 3tr missed in last row, 3ch, miss next 3tr, *1tr into each of next 3tr missed in last row, 3ch, miss next 3tr, rep from *, ending with 1dc under 3ch at end of row. Turn.
Last row forms check patt and is rep throughout, working in sequence of one row A, one row B and one row C. Cont in check patt until back measures 29cm from beg.
Armhole shaping
Break off all yarn and fasten off, then keeping to colour sequence as set throughout, cont as foll:
Next row Rejoin yarn with a ss to 3rd of first 3tr group of last row (i.e. 3ch and 2tr missed at beg of row), 1ch, 1tr into each of next 3tr missed in last row, work in patt to within last 2 groups of 3tr, 3ch, miss next 3tr, 1dc into next tr missed in last row. Turn. 6 sts decreased at each end of row. 116[122:128:134] sts.
Next row Work without shaping in patt, but working last dc into 1ch at end of row. Turn.
**Next row 3ch, miss first tr of first 3tr missed in last row and work 1tr into each of next 2tr, work in patt to end, ending with 2ch (instead of 3ch), 1dc under 3ch at end of row. Turn.
Rep last row once. One st decreased at each end of row. 114[120:126:132] sts.
Next row 3ch, miss first tr of first 2tr missed in last row and work 1tr into next tr, work in patt to end, ending with 1ch, 1dc under 3ch at end of row. Turn.
Rep last row once.** 112[118:124:130] sts.
Cont to dec one st at each end of every other row as foll:

Next 2 rows 3ch for turning ch, 3ch for first 3 sts, 1tr into each of next 3tr missed in last row, work in patt to end, missing last tr and ending with 1dc under 3ch at end of row. Turn.
Next 2 rows 3ch for turning ch, 2ch for first 2 sts, 1tr into each of next 3tr missed in last row, work in patt to last group of 3tr, 3ch, miss next 3tr, 1tr into each of next 2tr of 3tr missed in last row, 1dc under 3ch. Turn.
Next 2 rows 3ch for turning ch, 1ch for first st, 1tr into each of next 3tr missed in last row, work in patt to last group of 3tr, 3ch, miss next 3tr, 1tr into next tr of 2tr missed in last row, 1dc under 3ch. Turn.
Next 2 rows As 2nd patt row.
Rep from ** to **. 100[106:112:118] sts.
Cont without shaping as foll:
Next row 3ch, 1tr into first tr missed in last row, work in patt to end, ending with 1ch, miss last tr, 1dc under 3ch. Turn.
Rep last row until armhole measures 17[18:19:20]cm.
Neck and shoulder shaping
Next row Work in patt across first 18[21:24:27] sts. Turn, leaving rem sts unworked.
Cont in patt on these sts for first side of neck, dec one st at neck edge on next 3 rows. 15[18:21:24] sts.
Next row 3ch and work 1dc into each tr of last row and 1htr into each tr missed in last row. Fasten off.
Rejoin correct colour to rem sts at neck edge and work across centre 64 sts, working 1dc into each tr of last row and 1htr into each missed tr, then work in patt across last 18[21:24:27] sts. Complete as for first side of neck, reversing shaping.

▶ FRONT

Work as for back until armhole measures 3cm.
Divide for opening
Cont to work armhole shaping as for back *and at the same time* work in patt across next row until centre is reached, then turn, leaving rem sts unworked. Cont shaping armhole as for back, keeping centre edge straight until armhole shaping is complete. 50[53:56:59] sts.
If necessary work without shaping until armhole measures approx 9cm, ending at armhole edge.
Neck shaping
Next row Work in patt across first 34[37:40:43] sts. Turn, leaving 16 sts unworked.
Keeping to patt and keeping armhole edge straight, cont on these sts for first side of neck, dec 2 sts at neck edge on next and every row 5 times in all. Dec one st at neck edge on every row 9 times. 15[18:21:24] sts.
Work without shaping until front measures same as back to shoulder. Work last row as for back. Fasten off.
Rejoin correct colour to rem sts at side edge and work 2nd side of neck as for first side, reversing shaping. Using correct colour, finish off centre neck sts by working 1dc into each tr of last row and 1htr into each missed tr.

▶ MAKING UP

Press pieces on WS with damp cloth and warm iron. Sew shoulder and side seams. Using A and with RS facing, work one round of dc followed by one round of ss around neck edge, armholes and lower edge (see page 114). Press seams.

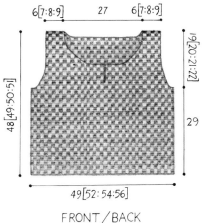

6[7:8:9]   27   6[7:8:9]

48[49:50:51]

19[20:21:22]

29

49[52:54:56]

FRONT / BACK

All measurements are in centimetres.

TEXTURED CHECKS

A smooth wool yarn and a knobbly cotton knop yarn in subtle shades combine to form an interesting textured check pattern on this casual loose-fitting sweater. The neck inset forms a collar or a polo neck.

▶ SIZES

To fit 81[86-91:96-102]cm/32[34-36:38-40]in bust.
Note: Figures for larger sizes are in square brackets. If there is only one set of figures, it applies to all sizes.
See diagram for finished measurements.

▶ MATERIALS

See page 118 for further yarn information
Use a lightweight wool yarn (approx 67m per 25g) and a lightweight cotton knop yarn (approx 75m per 50g):
125[150:200]g wool yarn in A (grey)
50[50:75]g wool yarn in C (coral)
125[150:175]g wool yarn in each of D (blue) and F (pale orange)
50g wool yarn in G (flesh)
125[125:150]g wool yarn in H (white)
350[400:450]g knop yarn in B (white)
250[300:350]g knop yarn in E (yellow)
4.50mm and 5.00mm crochet hooks *or size to obtain correct tension*
30cm zip fastener

▶ TENSION

17 sts to 10cm over check patt using 5.00mm hook for ss rows and 4.50mm hook for all other patt rows.
18 sts and 26 rows (unstretched rows) to 10cm over rib patt using 4.50mm hook.
Check your tensions before beginning.

Note: When using 2 colours in a row, carry yarn not in use across top of row below and work all sts over it. When changing colours in a row, always change to new colour with last yrh of previous htr (see page 112).
To check tension make 21ch and work base row as for back, then foll chart, working back and forth over first 20 sts. Read odd-numbered rows (RS) from right to left and even-numbered rows (WS) from left to right.

▶ BACK

Using smaller hook and A, make 91[95:99]ch.
Base row 1dc into 2nd ch from hook, 1dc into each ch to end. Turn. 90[94:98]dc.
1st row (RS) Using A, 2ch, 1htr into each of first 3 sts, yrh and insert hook into next st, yrh and draw a loop through, then using B, yrh and draw through all 3 loops on hook, carrying A across top of row below and working

sts over it, work 1htr in B into each of next 4 sts changing to A with last yrh of 4th htr, cont in this way working *4htr in A, 4htr in B, rep from * to last 2[6:2] sts, 1htr in A into each st to end. Turn.
2nd row Using A, 2ch, work 1htr in A into each htr in A and 1htr in B into each htr in B. Turn.
3rd row Using B, 2ch, work 1htr in B into each htr in A and 1htr in A into each htr in B. Turn.
4th row Using B, 2ch, work 1htr in B into each htr in B and 1htr in A into each htr in A. Turn.
5th and 6th rows As first and 2nd rows.
7th row Using C, 1ch, 1dc into each htr to end. Turn.
8th row Using larger hook and C, 1ch, work 1ss *very loosely* into each dc to end inserting hook under *both* loops at top of each dc. Turn.
9th row Using smaller hook and D, 2ch, 1htr into each of first 2ss changing to E with last yrh of 2nd htr, *2htr in E, 2htr in D, rep from * to end. Turn.
Cont with smaller hook until next ss row.
10th row Using E, 2ch, 2htr in E, *2htr in D, 2htr in E, rep from * to end. Turn.
11th and 12th rows As 9th and 10th rows.
13th and 14th rows Using A, as 7th and 8th rows.
15th row Using F, 2ch, 1htr into each of first 12ss changing to B with last yrh of 12th htr, *8htr in B, 12htr in F, rep from *, ending with 8[2:6]htr in B and 10[0:0]htr in F. Turn.
16th-18th rows 2ch, 1htr in B into each htr in B and 1htr in F into each htr in F. Turn.
19th and 20th rows Using G, as 7th and 8th rows.
21st and 22nd rows Using E for A and D for B, as first and 2nd rows.
23rd and 24th rows Using F, as 7th and 8th rows.
25th-38th rows As first-14th rows.
39th row Using B, 2ch, 1htr into each of first 8ss, changing to F with last yrh of 8th htr, *12htr in F, 8htr in B, rep from *, ending with 2[6:10]htr in F. Turn.
40th-42nd rows As 16th-18th rows.
43rd-48th rows As 19th-24th rows.
First-48th rows form patt. Cont in patt until back measures approx 68[69:70]cm from beg. Fasten off.

▶ FRONT

Work as for back until front measures approx 43[44:45]cm from beg.
Neck shaping
Next row Work in patt across first 45[47:49] sts. Turn, leaving rem sts unworked.
Keeping to patt as set, dec one st at neck edge on every foll htr row (do not dec on dc and ss rows) 18 times in all.

27[29:31] sts.
Note: For dec (yrh and insert hook into next st, yrh and draw a loop through) twice, yrh and draw through all 5 loops on hook — called 2htr tog.
Work in patt without shaping until there are same number of rows as back to shoulder.
Fasten off.

Work 2nd side of neck as for first side, reversing shaping.

▶ SLEEVES (make 2)

Using smaller hook and A, make 57[61:61]ch and work base row as for back. 56[60:60]dc.
1st row (RS) Using A, 2ch, *4htr in A, 4htr in B, rep from *, ending with 0[4:4] htr in A. Turn.
Keep to check patt as set on back *and at the same time* shape sides of sleeve, inc one st at each end of next row and then at each end of every alternate htr row (do not inc on dc and ss rows) 18 times in all. 92[96:96] sts.
Note: For inc work 2htr into first and last sts of row.
Cont in check patt until sleeve measures 39.5cm from beg. Fasten off.

▶ CUFFS (make 2)

Using smaller hook and H, make 31ch and work base row as for back. 30dc.
1st row 1ch, working into *back* loops only, 1dc into each dc to end. Turn.
Rep last row to form rib patt. Cont in rib patt until cuff measures 16[18:19]cm from beg unstretched.
Fasten off. Join cuff seam.

Using smaller hook and H, rejoin yarn with a ss to one end of cuff at seam, 3ch, work * 1tr into next row end, 2tr into next row end, rep from * all around, join with a ss to 3rd of 3ch. Fasten off.

▶ BACK RIB

Using smaller hook and H, make 8ch and work base and first rows as for cuffs. 7dc.
Cont in rib patt until rib, slightly stretched, fits across lower edge of back. Fasten off.

▶ FRONT RIB

Work as for back rib.

▶ POLO NECK COLLAR (3 pieces)

Fronts (make 2)
Using smaller hook and H, make 65ch and work base and first rows as for cuffs. 64dc.
Cont in rib patt, dec 2 sts at beg of next row (neck edge), dec 2 sts at neck edge on next 2 rows, *dec one st at neck edge on next 2 rows, dec 2 sts at neck edge on next row, rep from * 3 times more. 42dc. Dec one st at neck edge on next 2 rows. 40dc.
Next row Work in rib patt, dec 10 sts at straight side (collar edge) and 2 sts at neck edge. Turn. 28dc.
Dec one st at neck edge on next 2 rows. 26dc.

*Dec 2 sts at neck edge and one st at collar edge on next row, dec one st at neck edge on next 2 rows, rep from * 3 times more. 6dc. Fasten off.

Back collar
Using smaller hook and H, make 4ch and work base and first rows as for cuff. 3dc.
Work one row in rib patt. Cont in rib patt, *inc one st at beg of next row (collar edge), work 2 rows without shaping, *inc one st at collar edge on next row, work 2 rows without shaping, rep from * twice more. 7dc.
Next row 11ch, 1dc into 2nd ch from hook, 1dc into each of next 9ch, work in rib patt to end. Turn. 17dc.
Work 37 rows in rib patt without shaping.
Next row Work in ss across first 10dc, 1ch, work in rib patt to end. Turn. 7dc.
Complete 2nd side of collar as for first, reversing shaping.

▶ MAKING UP

Do not press. Join shoulder seams. Mark positions of sleeves 27[28:28]cm from shoulder seams. Sew on sleeves between markers. Sew back and front bands to lower edges of back and front. Join side and sleeve seams. Using smaller hook and H and with RS facing, work a row of dc evenly around neck edge, then work one round of ss inserting hook under both loops at top of each dc. Fasten off.
Join collar seams, leaving centre front open. Pin collar to neck, overlapping pullover body over collar approx 1.5cm and lining shoulder seams up with collar seams. Using H, sew collar in place stitching along neck edge just below neck edging.
Sew tr end of cuffs to inside of sleeves overlapping sleeve over cuff approx 5cm (adjusting length as required). Sew in zip.

DESIGN VARIATIONS

▶ PULLOVER WITH COLLAR

For a pullover with an ordinary collar, omit zip and turn back collar.

▶ V-NECK PULLOVER

For plain V-neck pullover omit collar.

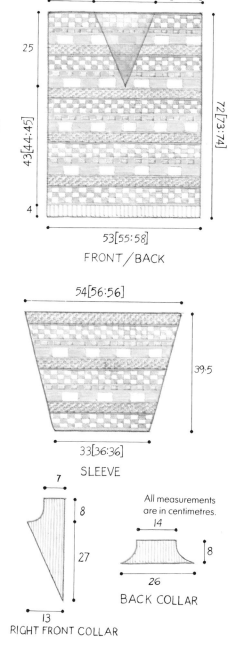

FRONT/BACK

SLEEVE

All measurements are in centimetres.

BACK COLLAR

RIGHT FRONT COLLAR

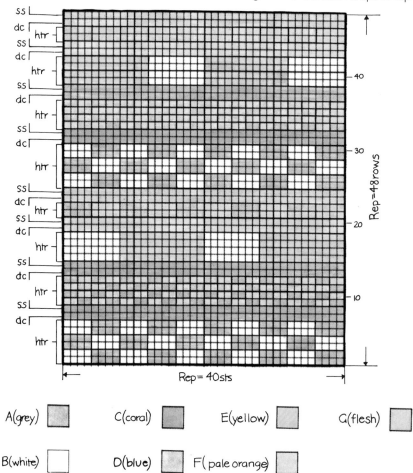

Rep= 48 rows

Rep = 40 sts

A(grey) ▢   C(coral) ▢   E(yellow) ▢   G(flesh) ▢

B(white) ▢   D(blue) ▢   F(pale orange) ▢

CHECK & PLAID

Sharply contrasting treble crochet checks and Tunisian crochet plaid produce this eyecatching sweater. The back and front are simple rectangular panels. Without sleeves, this design would make an attractive slipover.

▶ SIZES
To fit 81[86:91:96]cm/32[34:36:38]in bust.
Note: Figures for larger sizes are in square brackets. If there is only one set of figures, it applies to all sizes.
See diagram for finished measurements.

▶ MATERIALS
See page 118 for further yarn information
Use a fine wool tweed (approx 100m per 25g) and a lightweight cotton yarn (approx 185m per 50g):
150[175:200:200]g fine wool tweed in A (black)
100[100:125:125]g fine wool tweed in B (grey)
50[50:75:75]g fine wool tweed in C (grey green)
50g fine wool tweed in each of D (lilac)

and E (turquoise)
50g lightweight cotton yarn in each of F (cherry) and G (aqua green)
4.00mm crochet hook *or size to obtain correct tension*
5.50mm Tunisian crochet hook *or size to obtain correct tension*
Shoulder pads (optional)

▶ TENSION
20tr and 10½ rows to 10cm over check patt using 4.00mm hook.
19 sts and 23 loop rows to 10cm over Tunisian knit st stripe patt using 5.50mm Tunisian hook.
Check your tensions before beginning.

Note: Front and back are each made in 3 panels which are sewn tog. When working check patt with 2 colours, carry colour not in use loosely across top of row below and work all sts over it. When changing colours in a row of check patt, work last yrh of previous tr in new colour (see page 112). When changing colours on Tunisian knit st stripes, work last yrh of return row in new colour (see page 116).

▶ CENTRE BACK PANEL
Using crochet hook and A, make 35ch.
Base row Using A, 1tr into 5th ch from hook, 1tr into next ch, yrh and insert hook into next ch, yrh and draw a loop through, yrh and draw through 2 loops on hook, change to B, yrh and draw through 2 loops on hook to complete tr, carrying A loosely across top of row below and working all sts over it, work 4tr in B changing to A with last yrh of 4th tr, *4tr in A, 4tr in B, rep from * to end. Turn. 32 sts, counting 4ch as first st.
1st row Using B, 3ch to count as first tr, miss first tr, 1tr into each of next 3tr changing to A with last yrh of 3rd tr, 4tr in A, *4tr in B, 4tr in A, rep from *, working last tr into 4th of 4ch and

changing to B with last yrh of last st. Turn.
2nd row Using B; 3ch, miss first tr, 1tr into each of next 3tr changing to A with last yrh of 3rd tr, 4tr in A, *4tr in B, 4tr in A, rep from *, working last tr into 3rd of 3ch. Turn.
3rd row Using A, 3ch, miss first tr, 1tr into each of next 3tr changing to B with last yrh of 3rd tr, 4tr in B, *4tr in A, 4tr in B, rep from *, working last tr into 3rd of 3ch and changing to A with last yrh of last st. Turn.
4th row As 3rd row, but do not change to A at end of row.
5th row As 2nd row, but changing to C with last yrh of last st at end of row.
6th row As 2nd row, using C in place of B.
7th row As 3rd row, using C in place of B and changing to A at end of row.
8th row As 4th row.
9th row As 5th row, but changing to B with last yrh of last st at end of row.
2nd-9th rows form check patt. Cont in patt until panel measures 51[52:53:54]cm from beg. Fasten off.

▶ CENTRE FRONT PANEL
Work as for centre back panel.

▶ UNDERARM PANELS (make 2)
Using crochet hook and A, make 19[19:23:23]ch.
Base row Using A, 1tr into 5th ch from hook, 1tr into each of next 2ch, 4tr in B, 4tr in A, 4tr in B, 0[0:4:4]tr in A. Turn. 16[16:20:20] sts.
This sets position of checks. Cont in check patt as for back until panel measures 27[28:28:29]cm from beg. Fasten off.

▶ PLAID SIDE PANELS (make 4)
Using Tunisian hook and D, make 23[25:25:27]ch. Beg Tunisian knit st as foll:
Base row Insert hook into 2nd ch from hook, yrh and draw a loop through, *insert hook into next ch, yrh and draw a loop through, rep from * to end of ch. Do not turn at end of rows. 23[25:25:27] loops on hook.
1st row (return row) Yrh and draw through first loop on hook, *yrh and draw through 2 loops on hook, rep from * until there is one loop on hook (this forms first loop of next row).
2nd row (loop row) Miss first vertical loop in row below and insert hook from front to back through 2nd vertical loop (under the chain), yrh and draw a loop through, *insert hook through next vertical loop, yrh and draw a loop through, rep from * to end.
Note: To form a firm edge, insert hook through centre of last loop at the edge making sure that there are 2 vertical strands of yarn on hook at extreme left hand edge.
Last 2 rows form Tunisian knit st and

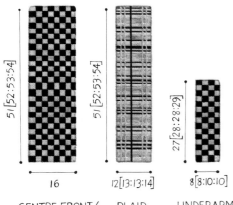

51[52:53:54] 51[52:53:54] 27[28:28:29]

16   12[13:13:14]   8[8:10:10]

CENTRE FRONT/   PLAID   UNDERARM
CENTRE BACK   PANEL   PANEL
PANEL

40[42:42:44]

24[24:25:25]

51[52:53:54]   27[28:28:29]

48[50:52:54]

FRONT/BACK
ASSEMBLED

All measurements are in centimetres.

48[48:50:50]

4

52   48

26[26:28:28]

SLEEVE

are rep throughout.
Cont in Tunisian knit st until 4 loop rows have been worked from beg (counting base row), ending with a return row and changing to A with last yrh of last return row. Cont in Tunisian knit st working in stripe sequence of **one loop row in A, one in E, 2 in A, one in F, one in A, 2 in G, 4 in D, 2 in E, one in D, one in A, one in D, one in F, one in D, one in A, 3 in E and 3 in D** and working all return rows in same colour as previous loop row. Rep from ** to ** to form stripe patt. Cont in stripe patt until panel measures 51[52:53:54]cm from beg, ending with a return row. Fasten off.

▶ **RIGHT SLEEVE**
Using crochet hook and A, make 55[55:59:59]ch.
Base row Using A, 1tr into 5th ch from

*8tr in B, 8tr in A, rep from *, ending last rep with 2[2:4:4]tr in A and working last tr into 4th of 4ch. Turn.
2nd row Using A, 3ch, 1tr into first tr (to inc one st), 1tr into each of next 1[1:3:3]tr, 8tr in B, *8tr in A, 8tr in B, rep from *, ending last rep with 1[1:3:3]tr in B, 2tr in B into 3rd of 3ch. Turn. 54[54:58:58] sts.
3rd row Using B, 3ch, miss first tr, 1tr into each of next 2[2:4:4]tr, 8tr in A, *8tr in B, 8tr in A, rep from *, ending last rep with 3[3:5:5]tr in A, working last tr into 3rd of 3ch and changing to B with last yrh of last tr. Turn.
4th row Using B, 3ch, 1tr into first tr, 1tr into each of next 2[2:4:4]tr, 8tr in A, *8tr in B, 8tr in A, rep from *, ending last rep with 2[2:4:4]tr in A, 2tr into 3rd of 3ch. Turn. 56[56:60:60] sts.
5th row Work in tr, working all sts in A in A and all sts in B in B.

iron, blocking to correct measurements.
Left front panel
Work vertical surface crochet stripes on a Tunisian panel as foll:
Using crochet hook and F and with RS facing, hold panel so that base row is at top, then beg at lower edge (last row of strip), insert hook from front to back between 3rd and 4th sts from right hand edge and into sp between first 2 return rows (chains), holding yarn at back of work throughout, yrh and draw a loop through, *keep loop on hook, insert hook through sp between next 2 return rows, yrh and draw a loop through sp and through loop on hook, rep from * up panel to end, working surface crochet loosely to avoid pulling pieces out of shape. Fasten off.

hook, 1tr into each of next 0[0:2:2]ch, 4tr in B, *4tr in A, 4tr in B, rep from *, ending last rep with 2[2:4:4]tr in B. Turn. 52[52:56:56] sts.
1st row Using B, 3ch, miss first tr, 1tr into each of next 1[1:3:3]tr, 4tr in A, *4tr in B, 4tr in A, rep from *, ending with 2[2:4:4]tr in A and working last tr into 4th of 4ch. Turn.
This sets position of checks. Cont in check patt as for back *and at the same time* inc one st at each end of next and every foll alternate row 22 times in all, working new sts into check patt. 96[96:100:100] sts.
Work in patt without shaping until sleeve measures 52cm from beg or desired sleeve length. Fasten off.

▶ **LEFT SLEEVE**
Using crochet hook and A, make 55[55:59:59]ch.
Base row Using A, 1tr into 5th ch from hook, 1tr into each of next 0[0:2:2]ch, 8tr in B, *8tr in A, 8tr in B, rep from *, ending last rep with 2[2:4:4]tr in B. Turn. 52[52:56:56] sts.
1st row Using B, 3ch, miss first tr, 1tr into each of next 1[1:3:3]tr, 8tr in A,

6th row As 5th row, but inc one st at each end of row. 58[58:62:62] sts.
7th row As 5th row.
8th row Work in tr, working all sts in B in A and all sts in A in B and inc one st at each end of row. 60[60:64:64] sts.
9th row As 5th row.
10th row As 5th row, but inc one st at each end of row. 62[62:66:66] sts.
11th row As 5th row.
12th row Work in tr, working all sts in B in A and all sts in A in C and inc one st at each end of row. 64[64:68:68] sts.
Cont in large check patt as set, working in checks of 8 sts and 4 rows and working in a sequence of 3 rows of these large checks using A and B and one row of large check using A and C *and at the same time* cont inc one st at each end of every alternate row and working new sts into large check patt until there are 96[96:100:100] sts. Complete as for right sleeve. Fasten off.

▶ **SURFACE CROCHET STRIPES**
Press four Tunisian crochet panels on WS with a damp cloth and a warm

Work 3 stripes more in F in the same way: one between 5th and 6th sts from right hand edge, one between 3rd and 4th sts from left hand edge and one between 5th and 6th sts from left hand edge.

Work one stripe in A in the same way between the 9th and 10th sts from the right hand edge.

Work 5 vertical stripes on a 2nd Tunisian crochet panel in the same way for right back.

Right front panel

Work vertical stripes in F as for left front panel. Then work stripe in A between 9th and 10th sts from left hand edge. Work a 2nd Tunisian crochet panel in the same way for left back.

▶ **MAKING UP**

Do not press check patt pieces. Darn in all loose ends. Join right and left front plaid panels to centre front check panel. Join 3 back panels in the same way. Join shoulder seams, leaving 27[27:28:28]cm open for neck. Sew side panels to back and front, beg seams at lower edge of pieces so that opening is left between shoulder and side panel for sleeve. Join sleeve seams, leaving 4[4:5:5]cm open at top of sleeve. Sew sleeves to armholes joining last 4[4:5:5]cm to top of side panel.

Edging

Using crochet hook and with RS facing, work a round of dc evenly around neck edge, using A along check patt and matching colour along Tunisian crochet. Then using A only, work one dc around stem of each dc from front (see page 110). Fasten off. Work an edging in the same way around lower edge of back and front. Using A and crochet hook, work 36dc evenly around cuff edge and complete as for other edgings. If desired, sew in shoulder pads.

DESIGN VARIATION

▶ **SLEEVELESS PULLOVER**

For sleeveless pullover follow instructions omitting sleeves. Edge armholes with a row of dc or work a strip of crochet rib (see page 114).

BUFFALO PLAID

This generously shaped jacket is worked in double crochet. The two-way pockets, which button down on top, are lined with fabric and open at the sides so they can be used as hand warmers.

▶ SIZE
One size only. To fit 86-96cm/34-38in bust.
See diagram for finished measurements.

▶ MATERIALS
See page 118 for further yarn information
Use a fine wool tweed yarn (approx 100m per 25g):
500g in A (gold)
550g in B (dark grey)
6.00mm crochet hook *or size to obtain correct tension*
62cm opened-ended zip fastener
4 buttons
Small amount of matching fabric for pocket lining
Dark grey sewing thread
Shoulder pads (optional)

▶ TENSION
14 sts and 15 rows to 10cm over plaid patt using 6.00mm hook and 2 strands of yarn held tog.
Check your tension before beginning.

Note: Plaid patt is worked with 2 strands of yarn held tog throughout. Back, front and sleeves are worked in rows which progress from side seam to side seam instead of from lower edge to top in the usual way.
When working with 2 colours in a row, carry colour not in use across top of row below, working all sts over it. Always change to new colour with last yrh of previous st (see page 112). For tension sample work in dc foll chart. Read odd-numbered rows (RS) from right to left and even-numbered rows (WS) from left to right.

▶ BACK
Using 2 strands of A, make 43ch and using 2 strands of each colour throughout, beg at side edge as foll:
Base row 1dc into 2nd ch from hook, 1dc into each of next 9ch, *(1dc in B into next ch, 1dc in A into next ch) 5 times*, 1dc in A into each of next 10dc, rep from * to * once more, 1dc in A into each of last 2ch. Turn. 42dc.
1st row 1ch, 1dc in A into each of first 2dc, *(1dc in B into next dc, 1dc in A into next dc) 5 times, 1dc in A into each of next 10dc, rep from * once more. Turn.
2nd row 1ch, *10dc in A, (1dc in B, 1dc in A) 5 times, rep from * once, ending with 2dc in A. Turn.

3rd and 4th rows Work in dc, using B only. Turn.
Rep first and 2nd rows twice more.
Armhole shaping
9th row Using B, make 43ch, 1dc in A into 2nd ch from hook, cont across ch and then across sts of last row, work 1dc in B, 1dc in A, 11dc in B, (1dc in A, 1dc in B) 5 times, *10dc in B, (1dc in A, 1dc in B) 5 times, rep from * to end. Turn. 84dc.
10th row 1ch, *(1dc in A, 1dc in B) 5 times, 10dc in B, rep from *, ending with (1dc in A, 1dc in B) twice. Turn.
11th row 1ch, (1dc in A, 1dc in B) twice, *10dc in B, (1dc in A, 1dc in B) 5 times, rep from * to end. Turn.
12th row As 10th row.
13th row Work in dc, using A only.
Shoulder shaping
14th row Work in dc, using A only and inc one st at end of row by working 2dc into last st. Turn.
15th row 1ch, 1dc in B, (1dc in A, 1dc in B) twice, *10dc in B, (1dc in A, 1dc in B) 5 times, rep from * to end. Turn.
16th row 1ch, *(1dc in A, 1dc in B) 5 times, 10dc in B, rep from *, ending with (1dc in A, 1dc in B) twice, 1dc in A. Turn.
Rep last 2 rows once more.
This sets plaid patt (see plaid chart). Keeping to plaid patt throughout, inc one st at beg of next row, work 5 rows without shaping, inc one st at beg of next row, work 5 rows without shaping. 87dc.
Neck shaping
Dec one st at beg of next row (neck edge) by working 2dc tog, then dec one st at neck edge on next 2 rows. 84 sts.
Work 10 rows without shaping, so ending with first of 2 rows in B. This is centre of back.
Beg with 2nd row in B, work 2nd half of back as for first, reversing shaping. Fasten off.

▶ LEFT FRONT
Using 2 strands of B, make 43ch and beg at side seam as foll:
Base row 1dc in A into 2nd ch from hook, 1dc in B into next ch, (1dc in A into next ch, 1dc in B into next ch) 4 times, 1dc in B into each of next 10ch, (1dc in A into next ch, 1dc in B into next ch) 5 times, 1dc in B into each of next 11ch, 1dc in A. Turn. 42dc.
1st row 1ch, 1dc in B, 1dc in A, *10dc in B, (1dc in A, 1dc in B) 5 times, rep from * once more. Turn.
2nd row 1ch, *(1dc in A, 1dc in B) 5 times, 10dc in B, rep from * once, ending with 1dc in B, 1dc in A. Turn.
3rd and 4th rows Work in dc, using A only. Turn.
Rep first and 2nd rows twice more.

Armhole shaping
9th row Using A, make 43ch, 1dc in A into 2nd ch from hook, cont across ch and then across sts of last row, work 3dc in A, *(1dc in B, 1dc in A) 5 times, 10dc in A, rep from * to end. Turn. 84dc.
Cont in plaid patt as set, working shoulder shaping as for back until 31 rows to neck (counting base row) have been completed, so ending at neck edge. 87dc.

Neck shaping

Keeping to plaid patt throughout, work neck shaping as foll:

Next row Work in ss across first 5dc, 1ch, work in patt to end. Turn. 82dc.

Next row Work in patt to last 2dc. Turn, leaving 2 sts unworked. 80dc. Dec one st at neck edge on next 3 rows, *work one row without shaping, dec one st at neck edge on next row, rep from * once more. 75dc. Work 4 rows more without shaping, so ending with first of 2 rows in A. Fasten off.

▶ RIGHT FRONT

Plaid patt is reversible, so that right front is worked exactly as for left front, but adding 3 more rows at centre front for overlap.

▶ SLEEVES (make 2)

Note: Incs for sleeve shaping are worked on every row so that separate lengths of ch need to be worked for every alternate row. Make 6 lengths of 4ch each in B and 3 lengths of 4ch each in A and set aside to be used during sleeve shaping.

Using 2 strands of B, make 10ch and beg at sleeve seam as foll:

Base row 1dc into 2nd ch from hook, 1dc into each of next 6ch, 1dc in A into next ch, 1dc in B into last ch. Turn. 9dc.

1st row 1ch, 1dc in A into first dc, 1dc in B into each of next 8dc, then using a separate length of 4ch in B, work 1dc in B into each of 4ch. Turn. 13dc.

2nd row 4ch in B, 1dc in A into 2nd ch from hook, then cont across rem 2ch and sts of last row work 1dc in B, 1dc in A, 11dc in B, 1dc in A, 1dc in B. Turn. 16dc.

3rd row 1ch, 1dc in A, 11dc in B, (11dc in A, 1dc in B) twice, then using a separate length of 4ch in B, work (1dc in A, 1dc in B) twice. Turn. 20dc.

4th row 4ch in A, using A only, work in dc across ch (beg in 2nd ch from hook) and across sts of last row. Turn. 23dc.

5th row Work in dc, using A only and working 4dc into length of 4ch in A. Turn. 27dc.

6th row 4ch in B, 1dc into 2nd ch from hook, then working across rem 2ch and sts of last row, 7dc in B, (1dc in A, 1dc in B) 5 times, 10dc in B, 1dc in A, 1dc in B. Turn. 30dc.

7th row 1ch, 1dc in A, 11dc in B, (1dc in A, 1dc in B) 5 times, 8dc in B, then using length of 4ch in B, work 2dc in B, 1dc in A, 1dc in B. Turn. 34dc.

8th row 4ch in B, 1dc in B into 2nd ch from hook, (1dc in A, 1dc in B) twice, 10dc in B, (1dc in A, 1dc in B) 5 times, 10dc in B, 1dc in A, 1dc in B. Turn. 37dc.

9th row 1ch, 1dc in A, 11dc in B, (1dc in A, 1dc in B) 5 times, 10dc in B, (1dc in A, 1dc in B) 4 times working across length of 4ch in B, 1dc in A in last ch. Turn. 41dc.

10th row 4ch in A, 1dc in B into 2nd ch from hook, 11dc in A, *(1dc in B, 1dc in A) 5 times*, 10dc in A, rep from * to * once, 2dc in A. Turn. 44dc.

Cont in plaid patt as set, (inc 4 sts at end of next row, inc 3 sts at beg of next row) 4 times more. 72dc.

Work without shaping until there are 54 rows along cuff edge (2 rows in A are at centre of sleeve).

Work 2nd side of sleeve as for first side, but reversing shaping. Fasten off.

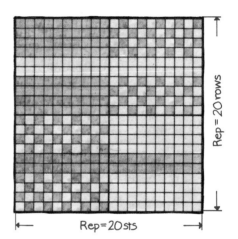

Rep = 20 rows

Rep = 20 sts

All measurements are in centimetres.

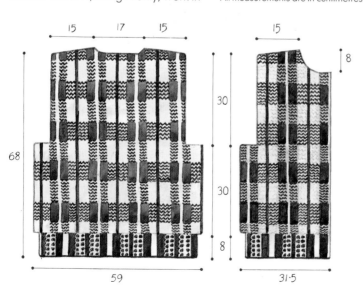

15 17 15

15

8

30

30

68

8

59

BACK

31·5

RIGHT FRONT

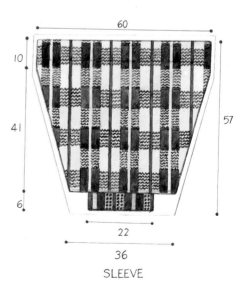

60

10

41

6

57

22

36

SLEEVE

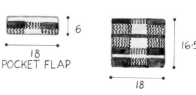

6

18

POCKET FLAP

16·5

18

POCKET

► **POCKETS** (make 2)
Using 2 strands of B, make 27ch.
Base row 1dc into 2nd ch from hook, 1dc into each of next 7ch, (1dc in A into next ch, 1dc in B into next ch) 5 times, 1dc in B into each of last 8ch. Turn. 26dc.
1st row 1ch, 8dc in B, (1dc in A, 1dc in B) 5 times, 8dc in B. Turn.
Rep last row twice more.
4th and 5th rows Work in dc, using A only. Turn.
Rep first row 4 times.
Cont in plaid patt as set until 25 rows have been worked from beg, counting base row. Fasten off.

► **POCKET FLAPS** (make 2)
Using 2 strands of A, make 27ch.
Base row 1dc into 2nd ch from hook, 1dc in B into next ch, *(1dc in A into next ch, 1dc in B into next ch)* 3 times, 1dc in A into each of next 10dc, rep from * to * 4 times. Turn. 26dc.
1st row 1ch, *(1dc in A, 1dc in B) 4 times*, 10dc in A, rep from * to * once. Turn.
2nd row As for first row of pocket.
3rd row (buttonhole row) 1ch, 4dc in B, 2ch in B, miss 2dc, 2dc in B, (1dc in A, 1dc in B) 5 times, 2dc in B, 2ch in B, miss 2dc, 4dc in B. Turn.
Cont in plaid patt as set, working in patt across 2ch in next row, until 9 rows have been worked from beg, counting base row. Fasten off.

► **HIP BAND**
Using 2 strands of B, make 13ch.
Base row 1dc into 2nd ch from hook, 1dc into each ch to end. Turn. 12dc.
1st-3rd rows Work in dc, using B only. Turn.
4th and 5th rows Work in dc, using A only. Turn.
6th-9th rows Work in dc, using B only. Turn.
10th-13th rows 1ch, (1dc in B, 1dc in A) 6 times. Turn.
14th-15th rows Work in dc, using B only. Turn.
16th-19th rows As 10th-13th rows.
20th-23rd rows As 6th-9th rows.
Rep 4th-23rd rows to form plaid patt.
Cont in patt until band measures 110cm from beg. Fasten off.

► **CUFFS** (make 2)
Using 2 strands of B, make 9ch.
Work base row as for hip band. 8dc.
Work in plaid patt as for hip band until cuff measures 22cm from beg. Fasten off.

► **COLLAR**
Join shoulder seams.
Using 2 strands of B, make 7ch and work base row as for hip band. 6dc.
Work in plaid patt as for hip band until collar fits around neck edge. Fasten off.

The sleeveless variation is shown here in a different plaid colourway.

► **MAKING UP**
Do not press. Pin top of sleeve to armhole so that jacket body overlaps sleeve by 5 rows. With RS facing work a backstitch seam between 5th and 6th rows through both thicknesses. Sew decreased edges of armhole to sides of sleeve.
Sew on cuffs, easing in fullness of sleeves. Join side and sleeve seams. Sew on hip band, easing in fullness of back and front. Sew collar in place at neck edge.
Using 2 strands of B and with RS facing, work dc evenly around 2 side edges and lower edge (foundation row) of each pocket.
Edgings
Using 2 strands of B and with RS facing, beg at right side seam and work dc along hip band to centre front, up right front, along collar edge, down left front and around hip band, working 2dc into each corner. Cont

around working 1ss into each dc of last round and inserting hook through both loops at top of each dc.
Work an edging in the same way around cuff edges and around 2 side edges and lower edge (foundation chain) of each pocket flap.
Cut lining for pockets 2cm larger all around than pocket. Turn under 1cm twice and stitch hem in place. Sew a pocket lining to back of each pocket leaving top open. Sew pockets and flaps to fronts, leaving side of pocket nearest side seam open. Sew top of fabric linings to fronts.
Sew in zip. Sew on buttons. Sew in shoulder pads if desired.

DESIGN VARIATION

► **SLEEVELESS JACKET**
For a sleeveless jacket omit sleeves and work dc and ss edging around armholes.

WOVEN PLAID

The comfortable soft feel of cotton chenille is perfect for an elegant lightweight jacket. Worked in a filet net of half treble, the vertical stripes are woven in afterwards by hand to produce the plaid design.

sps, counting first 4ch as first htr and 1ch sp.

1st row 3ch to count as first htr and 1ch sp, miss first htr, 1htr into next htr, *1ch, 1htr into next htr, rep from *, working last htr into 2nd of 4ch. Turn.

Keeping to stripe patt as set on back, beg shaping centre front edge as foll:
***Next row** Work in patt, ending with (1htr, 1ch, 1htr) all into 2nd of 3ch (thus inc one 1ch sp at centre front edge). Turn. 34[35:36:37] 1ch sps.
Work 5 rows in patt.***
Rep from *** to *** 5 times more.

▶ **SIZES**
To fit 81[86:91:96]cm/32[34:36:38]in bust.
Note: Figures for larger sizes are in square brackets. If there is only one set of figures, it applies to all sizes.
See diagram for finished measurements.

▶ **MATERIALS**
See page 118 for further yarn information
Use a lightweight cotton chenille yarn (approx 160m per 50g):
350[400:400:500]g in A (turquoise)
350[400:400:450]g in B (pink)
100[100:100:150]g in C (grey)
50[50:50:100]g in D (fuschia)
3.50mm crochet hook *or size to obtain correct tension*
Tapestry needle for weaving
2 buttons

▶ **TENSION**
Before weaving: 11 sps and 13½ rows to 10cm over filet patt using 3.50mm hook.
Check your tension before beginning.
After weaving: 11 sps and 14 rows to 10cm over woven filet patt.

Note: Jacket is worked in simple stripes of filet crochet. After all pieces are completed A and B are woven through spaces to create plaid effect. Weaving will slightly shorten pieces. Lengths of pieces after weaving are given on measurement diagram.

▶ **BACK**
Using A, make 115[119:123:127]ch.
Base row 1htr into 5th ch from hook, *1ch, miss next ch, 1htr into next ch, rep from * to end. Turn. 56[58:60:62] 1ch

2nd row As for first row, but working last htr into 2nd of 3ch.
Rep last row to form filet patt. Work one row more in A. Cont in stripe sequence of **5 rows B, one row C, 4 rows A, one row C, 2 rows B, one row D, one row B, one row C, 4 rows A.**
Cont in filet patt, rep stripe sequence from ** to ** until 43 rows have been worked from beg, counting base row.
Back measures approx 32cm.
Armhole shaping
Break off yarn, then keeping patt correct, miss first 6 sps and rejoin yarn to 7th htr of row with a ss, 3ch to count as first htr and 1ch sp, 1htr into next htr, work in patt over next 43[45:47:49] 1ch sps, turn leaving rem 6 sps unworked. 44[46:48:50] 1ch sps.
Cont in patt without shaping until 34[36:38:38] rows have been worked from beg of armhole.
Next row 1ch, 1ss into first htr, 1ss into ch, 1ss into next htr, 3ch, work in patt to last ch sp. Turn, leaving last ch sp unworked. 42[44:46:48] 1ch sps.
Rep last row once more. 40[42:44:46] 1ch sps. Fasten off. Armhole measures approx 27[28:29.5:29.5]cm.

▶ **LEFT FRONT**
Using A, make 69[71:73:75]ch and work base-2nd rows as for back. 33[34:35:36] 1ch sps.

Inc one 1ch sp at centre front edge on next row. 40[41:42:43] 1ch sps. Work in patt without shaping until there are same number of rows as back to armhole, so ending at armhole edge.

Neck and armhole shaping

Break off yarn, then keeping patt correct, miss first 6 sps and rejoin yarn to 7th htr of row with a ss, 3ch to count as first htr and 1ch sp, 1htr into next htr, cont in patt until 32[33:34:35] 1ch sps have been worked in all, turn leaving rem 2 sps unworked at neck edge.

Next row 1ch, ss over first 2 sps and into 3rd htr, 3ch, 1htr into next htr, work in patt to end. Turn. 30[31:32:33] 1ch sps.

Cont in patt keeping armhole edge straight and dec 2 sps at neck edge on next 2 rows, then dec one sp at neck edge on every row 6 times. 20[21:22:23] 1ch sps.

Work one row without shaping. Dec one sp at neck edge on next row and then on every foll alternate row 3 times more. 16[17:18:19] 1ch sps. Work 3 rows without shaping. Dec one sp at neck edge on next row and on every foll 4th row twice more. 13[14:15:16] 1ch sps.
Cont in patt without shaping until there are same number of rows as back, dec one sp at armhole edge on each of last 2 rows as for back. Fasten off.

▶ RIGHT FRONT
Filet patt is reversible, so work right front as for left front until 41 rows have been worked from beg, so ending at armhole edge. 40[41:42:43] 1ch sps.
Next row (buttonhole row) Work in patt over first 17[18:19:20] sps, *5ch, miss 3 sps, 1htr into next htr*, work in patt across next 15 sps, rep from * to *, work in patt to end. Turn.
Next row Work in patt to first 5ch, *(1ch, miss 1ch, 1htr into next ch) twice, 1ch, 1htr into next htr*, work in patt to next 5ch, rep from * to *, work in patt to end. Turn.
Complete as for left front.

▶ SLEEVE AND YOKE (make 2)
Using A, make 51[55:59:59]ch and work base-2nd rows as for back. 24[26:28:28] 1ch sps.
Next row 3ch, 1htr into first htr, cont in patt to end, ending with (1htr, 1ch, 1htr) all into 2nd of 3ch. Turn. 26[28:30:30] 1ch sps.
Keeping to patt as for back, work 2 rows without shaping. Inc one sp at each end of next row and then every foll 3rd row 4 times more. 36[38:40:40] 1ch sps. Work one row without shaping. Inc one sp at each end of next

row and then every foll alternate row 21 times more. 80[82:84:84] 1ch sps. Work 8 rows without shaping.
Yoke shaping
Break off yarn, then keeping patt correct, miss first 27[28:29:29] sps and rejoin yarn to 28th[29th:30th:30th] htr of row with a ss, 3ch to count as first htr and 1ch sp, 1htr into next htr, cont in patt until 26 sps have been worked in all, turn leaving rem 27[28:29:29] sps unworked.
Cont in patt on these centre sts, dec one sp at each end of next 2 rows. 22 sps.
Work 14[15:16:16] rows without shaping.
Neck shaping
Next row Work in patt over first 10 sps. Turn, leaving rem sts unworked.
Dec one sp at beg of next row. 9 sps. Work 9 rows in patt without shaping. Fasten off.

▶ WEAVING
Darn in all loose ends.
Back
Using 3 strands of B and tapestry needle and with RS of back facing, beg at lower right hand edge and weave in and out of first vertical row of ch sps working over and under chains between sps and leaving 15cm of yarn loose at edge for adjusting and fastening (see page 113). When armhole edge is reached, weave back down next vertical row of ch sps working *over* chains that were worked *under* in last row and vice versa until lower edge is reached. Cont in this way until 4[5:6:7] rows in B have been completed.
Cont in vertical rows from right to left across back, ***work 5 rows in A, 3

rows in B, 3 rows in A, 5 rows in B***, rep from *** to ***, ending with 4[5:6:7] rows in A.
If necessary adjust woven strands until length is correct. Darn in all loose ends.
Left front
Work as for back from ** to **. Then work in vertical stripe sequence as for back between *** and *** until centre front edge is reached. Darn in all loose ends.
Right front
Work as for left front but beg at side seam and working in rows from left to right reversing colours by working A for B and B for A.
Left sleeve and yoke
With RS of left sleeve facing and holding work so that cuff edge is at top, beg at right edge of sleeve and weave 0[1:2:2] vertical rows in A as for back. Then cont in vertical rows from right to left across sleeve and yoke, work *5 rows in B, 3 rows in A, 3 rows in B, 5 rows in A, rep from *, ending with 0[1:2:2] rows in B. Darn in all loose ends.
Right sleeve and yoke
With RS facing, work as for left sleeve and yoke.

▶ MAKING UP
Do not press. Join centre back yoke seam. Sew back and fronts to yoke and sleeves. Sew side and sleeve seams. Using A and with RS facing, beg at lower edge of right front and work dc evenly up right front, along back neck easing in to correct measurement, down left front and around lower edge, working 2dc into corners. Then work a round of ss, inserting hook under *both* loops at top of each dc. Fasten off. Sew on buttons.

All measurements are in centimetres.

MEASUREMENTS BEFORE WEAVING

40[42:43·5: 45·5]
27[28:29·5:29·5]
59[60:61·5:61·5] *
32
51[53:55:56·5]
BACK
*NOTE: AFTER WEAVING LENGTH OF BACK MEASURES 56·5[57·5:59:59]

19
12[13:13·5:14·5]
59[60:61·5:61·5] *
30[31:32:33]
LEFT FRONT
*NOTE: AFTER WEAVING LENGTH OF FRONT MEASURES 56·5[57·5:59:59]

26[27:28:28]   20   26[27:28:28]
8
8
21[21·5:22:22]
52·5
73·5[74:74·5:74·5] *
22[24:25:25]
SLEEVE AND YOKE
*NOTE: AFTER WEAVING LENGTH OF SLEEVE AND YOKE MEASURES 71[72:72·5:72·5]

TEXTURES

TEXTURES

There are many textures to be found in books of crochet stitches — anything from subtle raised stitches to high relief. The textured stitches chosen here are ones that allow scope for making your own pattern designs. Because the basic or background stitches used are simple ones, they can also be easily increased or decreased for garment shaping.

▶ **WORKING AROUND STEMS**

One method of creating a textured crochet fabric is by working around the stems of stitches instead of into the tops (see page 110). Two distinct textures are achieved — one by working around a stitch from the front and another by working around a stitch from the back. Pattern shapes are formed by contrasting these two textures. For example, either diagonal stripes (1) or diamonds (4) are possible replacements for the rectangular shapes in *Basketweave* (page 64).

▶ **BOBBLES**

Another way to make pattern shapes is by contrasting bobbles with a smoother background surface. Sample 2 gives an idea of the versatility of designing with bobbles. Any number of solid shapes or outlines could be made with bobbles in matching or contrasting colours and yarn textures.

Instead of bobble motifs, a more solid bobble texture may be preferred. The allover bobbles (3) worked in three colours would be effective in a chequerboard pattern. Large squares of plain double crochet could be alternated with large squares of bobbles — either striped or plain.

▶ **CABLES**

It is possible to imitate familiar and popular knitted Aran-type textures with crochet. Cables in crossed double trebles are especially appealing worked in mohair (see *Cables* on page 54) which emphasizes the depth of the stitches. Bobbles allow even more scope for variations. A simple way of making crochet cables is with surface slip stitch. On a smooth background or on a background of bobbles and coloured diamonds (5), intertwined surface slip stitch gives a credible cable substitute. The trick is to use a thick yarn or several strands of matching yarn for the slip stitch so that the cables gain prominence. Textured yarns also provide the bulk needed for cable shapes.

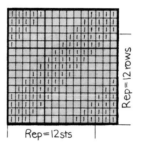

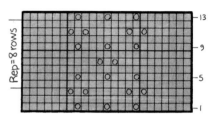

☐ bobble

☐ 1htr around stem from front
☐ 1htr around stem from back

1 Work first row in htr. Then work in htr following chart and begining and ending each row with 1dc.

2 Work odd-numbered rows in htr and even-numbered rows in tr, placing bobbles following chart. For bobble work (1htr, 3tr, 1htr), remove hook. Reinsert through top of first htr and draw loop through. Work 'cable' outline in surface ss.

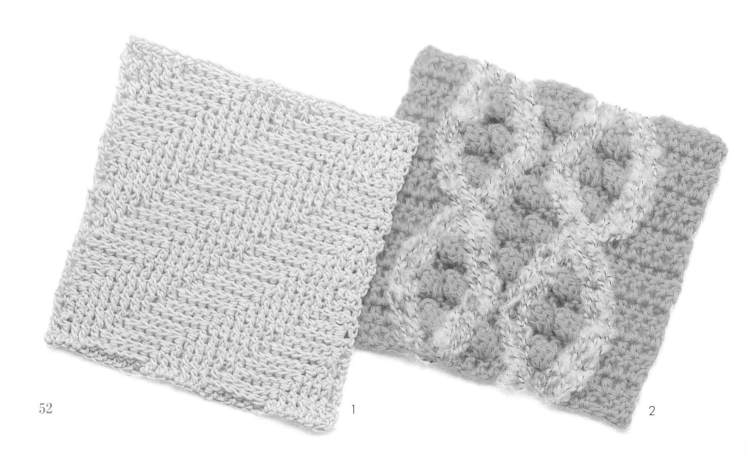

1

2

3 Use 3 colours A, B and C. Using A, make a multiple of 4ch.

Base row (RS) Using A, 1dc into 2nd ch from hook, 1dc into each ch. Turn.

1st row Using B, 1ch, 1dc into first dc, *leaving last loop of each st on hook work 2dtr into next dc, yrh and draw through all 3 loops on hook, 1dc into each of next 3dc, rep from *, ending last rep 1dc into each of next 2dc. Turn.

2nd row Using B, 1ch, 1dc into each st to end. Turn.

3rd row Using C, 1ch, 1dc into each of first 3dc, rep from * of first row, ending last rep 1dc into each of next 4dc. Turn.

4th row Using C, as 2nd row.

Rep first-4th rows to form patt, working in sequence of 2 rows each of C, B and A.

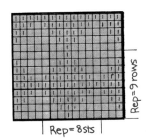

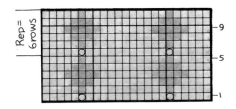

4 Follow chart and work as instructed for patt 1.

5 Follow chart and work as instructed for patt 2.

5

3

4

53

CABLES

Classic in shape, this V-neck mohair slipover has a surface design reminiscent of bold knitted Aran cables. It can be easily converted into a sweater by adding long sleeves. The cables are created by simply crossing double trebles. A further texture is added with bobbles.

▶ **SIZES**
To fit 81[86:91:96-102]cm/32[34:36: 38- 40]in bust.
Note: Figures for larger sizes are in square brackets. If there is only one set of figures, it applies to all sizes.
See diagram for finished measurements.

Sleeves are added for the design variation. The cables and bobbles are shown here worked in white on a pale blue background.

▶ **MATERIALS**
See page 118 for further yarn information
350[400:400:450]g of a lightweight mohair yarn (approx 155m per 50g)
4.50mm crochet hook *or size to obtain correct tension*

▶ **TENSION**
14 sts and 10 rows to 10cm over patt of one row htr and one row tr alternately using 4.50mm hook.
Check your tension before beginning.

▶ **BACK**
**Make 78[82:86:90]ch.
Base row** 1tr into 4th ch from hook, 1tr into each ch to end. Turn. 76[80:84:88] sts, counting turning ch as first st.
Beg rib as foll:

1st rib row 3ch to count as first tr, miss first tr, *yrh and insert hook from front to back and to front again around stem of next tr, yrh and draw a loop through, (yrh and draw through 2 loops on hook) twice — called 1tr front —, yrh and insert hook from back to front and to back again around stem of next tr, yrh and draw a loop through, (yrh and draw through 2 loops on hook) twice — called 1tr back —, rep from *, ending with 1tr into 3rd of 3ch. Turn.
Last row forms rib patt. Rep last row once more.
Beg cable patt as foll:
1st patt row (RS) 3ch to count as first tr, miss first tr, 1tr into each of next 7[9:10:12]tr, *miss next 2tr, 1dtr into next tr, 2dtr into next tr, then passing hook *behind* 3dtr just made, work 1dtr into first missed tr and 2dtr into 2nd missed tr, miss next 2tr, 1dtr into next tr, 2dtr into next tr, then passing hook in *front* of 3dtr just made, work 1dtr into first missed tr and 2dtr into 2nd missed tr*, 1tr into each of next 3tr, rep from * to * once, 1tr into each of next 22[22:24:24]tr, rep from * to * once, 1tr into each of next 3tr, rep from * to * once, 1tr into each of next 7[9:10:12]tr, 1tr into 3rd of 3ch. Turn.
92[96:100:104] sts.
2nd row 2ch to count as first htr, miss first tr, 1htr into each of next 7[9:10:12]tr, *1dc into each of next 12dtr, 1htr into each of next 3tr, 1dc into each of next 12dtr*, 1htr into each of next 22[22:24:24]tr, rep from * to * once, 1htr into each of next 7[9:10:12]tr, 1htr into 3rd of 3ch. Turn.
3rd row 3ch, miss first htr, 1tr into each of next 7[9:10:12]htr, *miss next 3dc, 1dtr into each of next 3dc, then passing hook in *front* of 3dtr just made, work 1dtr into first missed dc, 1dtr into 2nd missed dc and 1dtr into 3rd missed dc — called front cross or FC —, miss next 3dc, 1dtr into each of next 3dc, then passing hook *behind* 3dtr just made, work 1dtr into first missed dc, 1dtr into 2nd missed dc and 1dtr into 3rd missed dc — called back cross or BC —, 1tr into each of next 3htr, FC, BC*, 1tr into each of next 22[22:24:24]htr, rep from * to * once, 1tr into each of next 7[9:10:12]htr, 1tr into 2nd of 2ch. Turn.
4th row (WS) 2ch, miss first tr, 1htr into each of next 7[9:10:12]tr, *1dc into each of next 12dtr, 1htr into next tr, (1htr, 3tr, 1htr) all into next tr, remove hook from loop and reinsert into top of first htr of group of 5 sts just made, then draw last loop through and push group of sts through to RS of work — called bobble —, 1htr into next tr, 1dc into each of next 12dtr*, 1htr into each of next 22[22:24:24]tr, rep from * to * once, 1htr into each of next 7[9:10:12]tr, 1htr into 3rd of 3ch. Turn.
5th row 3ch, miss first htr, 1tr into each

of next 7[9:10:12]htr, *BC, FC, 1tr into each of next 3htr, BC, FC*, 1tr into each of next 22[22:24:24]htr, rep from * to * once, 1tr into each of next 7[9:10:12]htr, 1tr into 2nd of 2ch. Turn. 2nd-5th rows form cable patt. Rep 2nd- 5th rows 7 times more. Work 2nd patt row once. Back measures approx 37cm. Break off yarn and fasten off.**

Armhole shaping

Next row (RS) Miss first 7[9:10:12]htr and rejoin yarn to 8th[10th:11th: 13th]htr with a ss, 3ch to count as first tr, *FC, BC, 1tr into each of next 3htr, FC, BC*, 1tr into each of next 22[22:24:24]htr, rep from * to * once, 1tr into next htr. Turn, leaving rem sts unworked.

78[78:80:80] sts.

Next row 2ch to count as first htr, miss first tr, rep from * to * of 4th patt row once, 1htr into each of next 22[22:24:24]tr, rep from * to * once more, 1htr into 3rd of 3ch. Turn.

Next row 3ch to count as first tr, miss first htr, rep from * to * of 5th patt row once, 1tr into each of next 22[22:24:24]htr, rep from * to * once more, 1tr into 2nd of 2ch. Turn.

Cont in cable patt as set without shaping until 24[26:28:28] rows have been worked from beg of armhole, so ending with a 2nd[4th:2nd:2nd] patt row and working 8dc instead of 12dc across top of each of 4 cables in last row. Fasten off.

▶ **FRONT**

Work as for back from ** to **

Neck and armhole shaping

Next row (RS) Miss first 7[9:10:12]htr and rejoin yarn to 8th[10th:11th: 13th]htr with a ss, 3ch to count as first tr, *FC, BC, 1tr into each of next 3htr, FC, BC*, 1tr into each of next 9[9:10:10]htr, (yrh and insert hook into next htr, yrh and draw a loop through,

yrh and draw through 2 loops on hook) twice, yrh and draw through all 3 loops on hook — called 2tr tog. Turn, leaving rem sts unworked.

38[38:39:39] sts.

Next row 2ch to count as first htr, miss first tr, 1htr into each of next 9[9:10:10]htr, rep from * to * of 4th patt row once, 1htr into 3rd of 3ch. Turn.

Next row 3ch to count as first tr, miss first htr, rep from * to * of 5th patt row once, 1tr into each of next 8[8:9:9]htr, 2tr tog (working last tr of 2tr tog into 2nd of 2ch). Turn. 37[37:38:38] sts.

Work one row in patt without shaping. Keeping armhole edge straight, cont in cable patt dec one st at neck edge on next row and then on every other row until 29[29:30:30] sts rem.

Cont in patt without shaping until there are same number of rows as back to shoulder, working 8dc instead of 12dc across top of each of 2 cables in last row. Fasten off.

With RS facing rejoin yarn with a ss to first htr (centre front) of row where neck shaping was begun, 3ch, 2tr tog, 1tr into each of next 8[8:9:9]htr, *FC, BC, 1tr into each of next 3htr, FC, BC*, 1tr into next htr, turn, leaving rem 7[9:10:12] sts unworked.

38[38:39:39] sts.

Complete right side of neck as for left side, reversing shaping.

▶ **ARMHOLE BANDS**

Join shoulder and side seams. With RS facing and beg at side seam, join yarn to armhole edge with a ss, 3ch to count as first tr, work 6[8:9:11]tr evenly along armhole shaping to corner, 1dtr into corner, work 73[79:85:85]tr evenly along straight edge of armhole, 1dtr into corner, 7[9:10:12]tr along armhole shaping to side seam, join with a ss to 3rd of 3ch, do not turn.

89[99:107:111] sts.

Beg rib as foll:

1st round 3ch, *1tr front, 1tr back, rep from * to end, join with a ss to 3rd of 3ch. Do not turn.

Rep last round once more and fasten off.

▶ **MAKING UP**

Do not press. With RS facing and beg at right shoulder seam, work a round of dc evenly around neck edge, then work 2 rounds more working 1dc around stem of each dc from front (see page 114). Fasten off. Edging will roll to RS.

DESIGN VARIATION

▶ **PULLOVER WITH SLEEVES**

For a pullover with sleeves make back and front as for sleeveless pullover. For sleeves make 28[31:34:34]ch and work base row as for back. 26[29:32:32] sts. Work 2 rows in rib as for back.

Next row 3ch to count as first tr, miss first tr, *2tr into next tr, rep from *, 1tr into 3rd of 3ch. Turn.

50[56:62:62] sts.

Next row 2ch to count as first htr, miss first tr, *1htr into next tr, rep from *, 1htr into 3rd of 3ch. Turn.

Next row 3ch, miss first htr, *1tr into next htr, rep from *, 1tr into 2nd of 2ch. Turn.

Last 2 rows form patt. Cont in patt inc one st at each end of next row and every foll 4th row 8 times.

68[74:80:80] sts.

Cont in patt without shaping until sleeve measures 49cm from beg. Fasten off.

Join shoulder seams. Sew sleeves to armholes. Join side and sleeve seams. Make up as for sleeveless version.

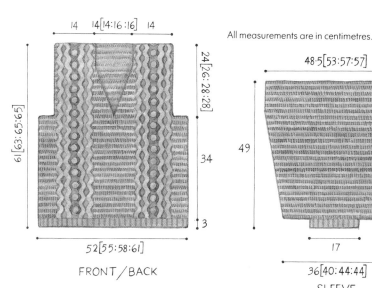

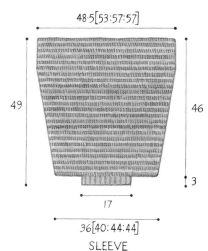

All measurements are in centimetres.

FRONT/BACK

14   14[14:16:16]   14

24[26:28:28]

61[63:65:65]

34

3

52[55:58:61]

48·5[53:57:57]

49

46

3

17

36[40:44:44]

SLEEVE

ZIGZAGS

This backless top with long sleeves is worked in half treble. A deep crochet rib fits the waist snuggly and bobbles form zigzag panels down both sides of the front and back.

► SIZES

To fit 81[86:91:96]cm/32[34:36:38]in bust.

Note: Figures for larger sizes are in square brackets. If there is only one set of figures, it applies to all sizes. *See diagram for finished measurements.*

► MATERIALS

See page 118 for further yarn information
400[400:450:450]g of a fine slubbed cotton and linen yarn (approx 170m per 50g)
4.00mm crochet hook *or size to obtain correct tension*
Shoulder pads

► TENSION

18htr and 15½ rows to 10cm using 4.00mm hook.
20dc and 21 rows slightly stretched over rib patt using 4.00mm hook.
Check your tensions before beginning.

Note: Body is worked in one piece to armholes and then divided for backs and front.

► BODY

Make 29[31:31:33]ch and beg rib as foll:
Base rib row 1dc into 2nd ch from hook, 1dc into each ch to end. Turn. 28[30:30:32]dc.
1st rib row 1ch, working into *back* loops only, 1dc into each dc to end. Turn.
Rep last row to form rib patt. Cont in rib patt until 135[143:151:157] rows have been worked from beg, counting base row. Fasten off.
Turn rib sideways and work sts for body along rib row ends as foll:
Rejoin yarn with a ss to end of foundation row, 2ch, 2htr into same place as ss, 1htr into each of next 2[4:5:6] row ends, (2htr into next row

end, 1htr into each of next 5 row ends) 4 times, *2htr into next row end, 1htr into each of next 0[1:2:3] row ends, 2htr into next row end, 1htr into each of next 1[2:3:4] row ends*, (2htr into next row end, 1htr into each of next 2 row ends, 2htr into next row end, 1htr into each of next 3 row ends) 9 times, rep from * to * once, (2htr into next row end, 1htr into each of next 5 row ends) 4 times, 2htr into next row end, 1htr into each of next 1[3:4:5] row ends, turn leaving rem 13[13:15:15] row ends unworked. 154[162:168:174]htr.
Next row 2ch, working into *both* loops throughout, 1htr into each htr to end. Turn.
Beg bobble patt as foll:
1st patt row (RS) 2ch, 1htr into each of first 1[1:2:2]htr, *(1htr, 3tr, 1htr) all into next htr, remove hook from loop and reinsert into top of first htr of group of 5 sts just made, then draw last loop through — called bobble —, (1htr into next htr, 1 bobble into next htr) 3 times*, 1htr into each of next 47[51:51:53]htr, rep from * to * once, 1htr into each of next 30[30:34:36]htr, rep from * to * once, 1htr into each of next 47[51:51:53]htr, rep from * to * once, 1htr into each of last 1[1:2:2]htr. Turn. 154[162:168:174] sts.
2nd and all WS rows 2ch, 1htr into each htr and each bobble to end. Turn.
3rd row 2ch, 1htr into each of first 5[5:6:6]htr, *1 bobble into next htr, (1htr into next htr, 1 bobble into next htr) 3 times*, 1htr into each of next 39[43:43:45]htr, rep from * to * once, 1htr into each of next 38[38:42:44]htr, rep from * to * once, 1htr into each of next 39[43:43:45]htr, rep from * to * once, 1htr into each of last 5[5:6:6]htr. Turn.
5th row 2ch, 1htr into each of first 9[9:10:10]htr, *1 bobble into next htr, (1htr into next htr, 1 bobble into next htr) 3 times*, 1htr into each of next 31[35:35:37]htr, rep from * to * once,

1htr into each of next 46[46:50:52]htr, rep from * to * once, 1htr into each of next 31[35:35:37]htr, rep from * to * once, 1htr into each of last 9[9:10:10]htr. Turn.
7th row 2ch, 1htr into each of first 13[13:14:14]htr, *1 bobble into next htr, (1htr into next htr, 1 bobble into next htr) 3 times*, 1htr into each of next 23[27:27:29]htr, rep from * to * once, 1htr into each of next 54[54:58:60]htr, rep from * to * once, 1htr into each of next 23[27:27:29]htr, rep from * to * once, 1htr into each of last 13[13:14:14]htr. Turn.
9th row As 5th row.
11th row As 3rd row.
12th row As 2nd row.
First-12th rows form bobble patt. Cont in bobble patt until body measures 17cm from rib, ending with a WS row.
Left back and armhole shaping
Next row Work in patt over first 27[29:30:31]htr. Turn, leaving rem 127[133:138:143] sts unworked.
Next row 1ch, 1ss into each of first 2htr (armhole edge), 2ch, work in patt to end. Turn. 25[27:28:29]htr.
Keeping to patt, dec one st at armhole edge on next row and on every foll row 1[2:2:3] times more. 23[24:25:25] sts.
Note: To dec one st at end of row work to last 2 sts, (yrh and insert hook into next st, yrh and draw a loop through) twice, yrh and draw through all 5 loops on hook — called 2htr tog. To dec one st at beg of row work 2htr tog over first 2 sts.
Work one row without shaping. Dec one st at armhole edge on next row.
Rep from ** to ** once more. 21[22:23:23] sts.
Cont in patt without shaping until armhole measures 20[21:22:23]cm, ending with a WS row. Fasten off.
Front and armhole shaping
With RS facing, return to rem sts and miss next 9 sts on body (after left back), rejoin yarn to next st with a ss, 2ch, 1htr

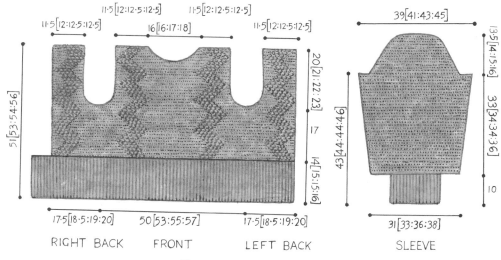

RIGHT BACK   FRONT   LEFT BACK   SLEEVE

All measurements are in centimetres.

into same place as ss, keeping to patt as set work across next 81[85:89:93]htr, turn leaving rem 36[38:39:40]htr unworked. 82[86:90:94] sts.

Next row 1ch, 1ss into each of first 2htr, 2ch, work in patt across next 78[82:86:90] sts. Turn, leaving rem 2 sts unworked.

Keeping to patt, dec one st at each end of next row and on every foll row 1[2:2:3] times more. 74[76:80:82] sts.

Work one row without shaping. Dec one st at each end of next row.

Rep from *** to *** once more. 70[72:76:78] sts.

Cont in patt until front has 7 rows less than left back, so ending with a RS row.

Front neck shaping

Next row (WS) Work in patt across first 26[27:28:28] sts. Turn, leaving rem 44[45:48:50] sts unworked.

Next row (RS) 1ch, 1ss into each of first 2htr (neck edge), work in patt to end. Turn. 24[25:26:26] sts.

Keeping to patt, dec one st at neck edge on next row and on every foll row twice more. 21[22:23:23] sts.

Work 2 rows without shaping. Fasten off.

With WS facing, return to rem sts at centre front and miss next 18[18:20:22] sts for centre front neck, rejoin yarn to next st with a ss, 2ch, 1htr into same place as ss, work in patt across rem 25[26:27:27] sts, turn. 26[27:28:28] sts.

Complete 2nd side of neck as for first side, reversing shaping.

Right back and armhole shaping

With RS facing, miss next 9 sts on body (after front) and rejoin yarn to next st with a ss, 2ch, 1htr into same place as ss, work in patt across rem

26[28:29:30] sts, turn. 27[29:30:31] sts.

Complete right back as for left back, reversing shaping.

▶ **SLEEVES** (make 2)

Make 21ch and work base and first rib rows as for body rib. 20dc.

Cont in rib patt as for body rib until 32[34:36:38] rows have been worked from beg, counting base row. Do not fasten off.

Turn rib sideways and work sts for sleeve along rib row ends as foll: 2ch, 2htr into each of first 4[5:6:7] row ends, (1htr into next row end, 2htr into each of next 2 row ends) 8 times, 2htr into each of last 4[5:6:7] row ends, turn. 56[60:64:68]htr.

Next row 2ch, working into *both* loops throughout, 1htr into each htr to end. Turn.

Rep last row once more.

Next row 2ch, 2htr into first htr, 1htr into each htr to last htr, 2htr into last htr. Turn. 58[62:66:70]htr.

Work 4 rows in htr without shaping. Inc one st at each end of next row.

Rep from * to * 5 times more. 70[74:78:82] sts.

Cont in htr without shaping until sleeve measures 43[44:44:46]cm from beg, including rib.

Top of sleeve shaping

Next row 1ch, 1ss into each of first 5htr, 2ch, 1htr into each htr to last 5htr. Turn, leaving rem 5htr unworked. 60[64:68:72]htr.

Cont in htr, dec one st at each end of next and every foll row 17[18:19:21] times in all. 26[28:30:30]htr.

Dec 2 sts at each end of next and every foll row 3 times in all. 14[16:18:18]htr. Fasten off.

▶ **MAKING UP**

Do not press. Join shoulder seams. Join cuff and sleeve seams. Set in sleeves, easing in fullness at top. Join rib seam at back.

With RS facing, work dc evenly up left back, along front neck, down right back and along top of ribbing (easing tog ribbing slightly) to left back, cont around working 1dc around stem of each dc from front (see page 114) to end of round. Fasten off.

Sew in shoulder pads.

CLUSTERS

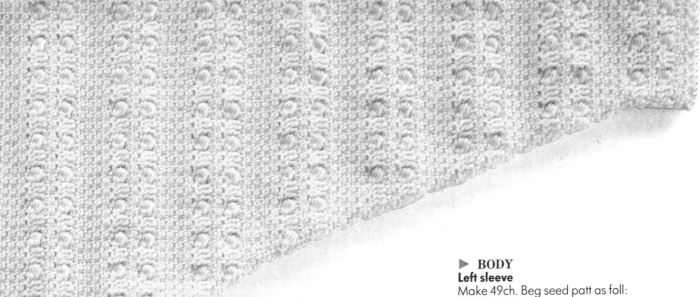

The revealing neckline, the crisp collar and fitted cuffs on this classic evening top are all edged with small pearl beads. Cluster stitches in a silk and wool yarn form a softly textured surface on the sleeves.

▶ **SIZES** To fit 86[91]cm/34[36]in bust.
Note: Figures for larger size are in square brackets. If there is only one set of figures, it applies to both sizes. *See diagram for finished measurements.*

▶ **MATERIALS**
See page 118 for further yarn information
625g of a lightweight wool and silk yarn (approx 95m per 25g)
4.00mm crochet hook *or size to obtain correct tensions*
One button
3mm pearl beads (approx 500)
Matching sewing thread
Beading needle

▶ **TENSION**
27 sts and 28 rows to 10cm over seed patt using 4.00mm hook.
14 row rep of cluster patt measures 6.5cm using 4.00mm hook.
Check your tensions before beginning.

Note: Garment is worked in one piece from cuff edge to cuff edge.

▶ **BODY**
Left sleeve
Make 49ch. Beg seed patt as foll:
Base row 1dc into 3rd ch from hook, *1ch, miss 1ch, 1dc into next ch, rep from * to end. Turn. 48 sts, counting each dc, each ch sp and 2 turning ch as one st.
1st row 2ch, 1dc into first ch sp, * 1ch, 1dc into next ch sp, rep from *, ending with 1ch, 1dc into 2ch sp at end. Turn. Last row forms seed patt.
2nd and 3rd rows Rep first row twice more.
4th row 3ch to count as first tr, 1tr into first ch sp, 1tr into next dc, 1tr into next ch sp, 1tr into next dc, *1ch, miss next ch sp, 1tr into next dc, (yrh and insert hook from front to back and to front again around stem of tr just made, yrh and draw a loop through, yrh and draw a loop through first 2 loops on hook) 4 times, yrh and draw through all 5 loops on hook — called cluster —, 1ch, miss next ch sp, 1tr into next dc, 1tr into next ch sp, 1tr into next dc*, rep from * to *, ending with 1tr into 2ch sp. Turn.
5th row 2ch, miss first tr, 1dc into next tr, 1ch, miss next tr, 1dc into next tr, *1ch, 1dc into top of bobble, 1ch, 1dc into next tr, 1ch, miss 1tr, 1dc into next tr*, rep from * to *, ending with 1ch, miss next tr, 1dc into 3rd of 3ch. Turn.
6th and 7th rows Rep first row twice.
8th and 9th rows As 4th and 5th rows.
Left sleeve shaping
Beg shaping sleeve as foll:
10th row 1ch, 1dc into first dc, 1ch, 1dc into first ch sp, *1ch, 1dc into next ch sp, rep from *, ending with 1ch, 2dc into 2ch sp at end. Turn. 50 sts.

11th row 1ch, 1dc into first dc, 1ch, miss next dc, 1dc into first ch sp, *1ch, 1dc into next ch sp, rep from *, 1dc into last dc. Turn.

12th row 2ch, 1dc into first dc, 1ch, miss next dc, 1dc into first ch sp, *1ch, 1dc into next ch sp, rep from *, ending with 1ch, 1dc into last dc. Turn. 52 sts.

13th row As first row.

14th-17th rows As 10th to 13th rows. 56 sts.

18th row 3ch to count as first tr, 1tr into first dc, 1tr into first ch sp, 1tr into next dc, rep from * to * of 4th row, working last 2tr of last rep into 2ch sp at end. Turn. 58 sts, counting each cluster, each tr and each ch sp.

19th row 1ch, 1dc into first tr, 1ch, miss next tr, 1dc into next tr, rep from * to * of 5th row, ending with 1dc into 3rd of 3ch. Turn.

20th and 21st rows As 12th and 13th rows. 60 sts.

22nd row 3ch, 1tr into first dc, 1tr into first ch sp, 1tr into next dc, 1tr into next ch sp, 1tr into next dc, rep from * to * of 4th row, ending with 2tr into 2ch sp at end. Turn. 62 sts.

23rd row 1ch, 1dc into first tr, (1ch, miss next tr, 1dc into next tr) twice, rep from * to * of 5th row, ending with 1ch, miss next tr, 1dc into next tr, 1dc into 3rd of 3ch. Turn.

Cont in this way inc one st at each end of next and every foll alternate row *and at the same time* keeping to cluster patt of 9 rows seed patt, one cluster row, 3 rows seed patt, one cluster row until 5 pairs of cluster rows have been worked from beg, then work 8 rows in seed patt still inc one st at each end of every alternate row. 112 sts.

Note: As sleeve widens add clusters, keeping patt correct and lining clusters up with clusters in previous rows.

Cont in cluster and seed patts as set, inc one st at each end of next row and every foll row until 8 pairs of cluster rows have been worked from beg, then work 7 rows in seed patt still inc one st at each end of every row. 194 sts. Break off yarn and set piece aside.

Front hip extension

Make 19[23]ch and work base row as for beg of cuff. 18[22] sts.

1st inc row (RS) 2ch, 1dc into first dc, 1ch, 1dc into first ch sp, work in seed patt to end. Turn. 20[24] sts.

2nd inc row Work in seed patt to end, ending with 1dc, 1ch, 1dc all into 2ch sp. Turn. 22[26] sts.

Rep last 2 rows 3 times more. 34[38] sts.

Break off yarn and fasten off.

Back hip extension

Make 19ch and work base row as for beg of cuff. 18[22] sts.

1st inc row As 2nd inc row of front hip extension. 20[24] sts.

2nd inc row As first inc row of front hip extension. 22[26] sts.

Rep last 2 rows 3 times more. 34[38] sts.

Do not break off yarn.

Joining

Using a separate ball of yarn, make one length of 23[25]ch and one length of 25[27]ch and set aside for next row. Join hip extensions to sleeve as foll: With RS of back hip extension facing, work in seed patt to end of piece, 1ch, 1dc into first ch of length of 23[25]ch, *1ch, miss next ch, 1dc into next ch*, rep from * to * across ch, 1ch, with RS

of sleeve facing work 1dc into first dc, miss 2nd of first 2dc at beg of row, 1ch, 1dc into first ch sp, cont in seed patt to end of sleeve, 1ch, miss 1dc at end of row, 1dc into first ch of length of 25[27]ch, rep from * to * across ch, with RS of front hip extension facing work 1dc into first ch sp, work in seed patt to end. Turn. 312[324] sts.

Work one row in seed patt.

Work one cluster row, 3 seed patt rows and one cluster row.

Cont in seed patt only, work 25[27] rows more, so ending with a WS row.

Back neck shaping

Next row (RS) Work in seed patt across first 154[160] sts. Turn, leaving rem sts unworked.

Cont on these sts only, dec one st at beg of next row (neck edge). Dec one st at neck edge on next row and then on every foll alternate row twice more. 150[156] sts.

Work 26 rows without shaping, so ending with a RS row.

Inc one st at beg of next row (neck edge). Work one row without shaping. Rep last 2 rows once more.

Inc one st at neck edge on next 2 rows. 154[160] sts.

Break off yarn and fasten off.

Front neck shaping

With RS facing, miss 11 sts on row where back neck shaping began and rejoin yarn to next st (a ch sp) with a ss, 1ch, 1dc into same place as ss was worked, work in patt to end of row, turn. 147[153] sts.

Dec 2 sts at end of next row (front neck edge), dec one st at neck edge on next 5 rows. Work one row without shaping, so ending with a WS row.

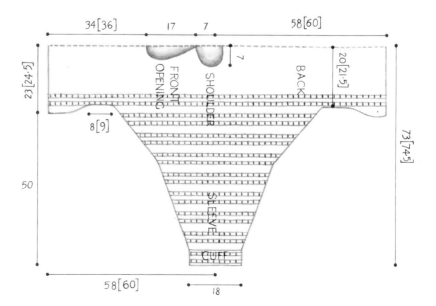

Lower neckline shaping

Dec one st at beg of next row (RS) and work in patt until there are 23 sts, turn leaving rem sts unworked.

Cont on these sts only, dec 2 sts at beg (lower neckline edge) of next row.

Dec one st at beg (neck edge) of next row and 2 sts at end of row.

Keeping neck edge straight, dec 2 sts at lower neckline edge on every row until 2 sts rem. Fasten off.

To complete lower neckline edge, return to row where lower neckline shaping began and with RS facing miss next 19 sts, rejoin yarn with a ss to next st (ch sp), 1ch, 1dc into same place as ss, work in patt to end of row, turn. 100[106] sts.

Dec one st at end of next row (neckline edge). Dec one st at neckline edge on next 3 rows.

Work one row without shaping. Dec one st at neckline edge on next row. 92[98] sts.

Work 10 rows without shaping.

Inc one st at neckline edge on next row. Work one row without shaping. Inc one st at neckline edge on next 4 rows, so ending with a RS row. 100[106] sts. Do not break off yarn.

Beg shaped piece for right front neck as foll:

Using a separate ball of yarn, make 3ch and work base row in dc. 2dc.

Next row (WS) 2ch, 1dc into first dc, 1ch, 1dc into next dc. Turn. 4 sts.

Cont in seed patt inc 2 sts at end (neckline edge) of next row. Inc 2 sts at neckline edge on next 6 rows, so ending with a RS row. 18 sts.

Inc 2 sts at beg (neckline edge) of next row and one st at end (neck edge) of row. Inc 2 sts at neckline edge on next row. 23 sts.

Break off yarn and fasten off.

Make a length of 19ch and set aside for next row.

Return to last row worked on body and with WS facing work from lower edge of front to neckline edge, work across 19ch, then cont in patt across shaped piece for right front neck, inc one st at end of row (neck edge). 140[146] sts.

Work one row without shaping.

Inc one st at neck edge on next 5 rows. Inc 2 sts at neck edge on next row, so ending with a RS row. 147[153] sts. Do not break off yarn.

Joining front and back

Using a separate ball of yarn, make a length of 11ch and set aside for next row.

With WS facing, beg at lower front edge and work in patt to front neck edge, work in patt across 11ch, then with WS of back facing work in patt across back. 312[324] sts.

Work 24[26] rows in seed patt, so ending with a WS row. Work one cluster row, work 3 rows in seed patt, work one cluster row, work 2 rows in

seed patt, so ending with a RS row.

Right front hip shaping

Next row Work in patt across first 34[38] sts. Turn, leaving rem sts unworked.

Dec 2 sts at beg of next row. Then keeping lower edge of front straight, dec 2 sts at same edge as last dec on next 7 rows. 18[22] sts. Fasten off.

Right back hip shaping

With WS facing, rejoin yarn to back and work across last 34[38] sts of row. Dec 2 sts at end of next row. Then keeping lower edge of back straight, complete shaping as for right front hip shaping. Fasten off.

Right sleeve

With WS facing, return to last row of body where hip shaping began, miss first 25[27] sts and work in patt across centre 194 sts.

Keeping to patt as set for left sleeve, dec one st at each end of every row 42 times.

Work one row without shaping. Dec one st at each end of next row.

Rep last 2 rows 30 times more. 48 sts. Work 9 rows without shaping. Fasten off.

▶ COLLAR

Make 121ch and work base and first rows as for beg of left cuff. 120 sts. Cont in seed patt until 10 rows have been worked from beg, counting base row.

Next row 1ch, miss first dc, 1dc into next ch sp, *miss next dc, 1dc into next ch sp, rep from * to end.
Fasten off.

▶ MAKING UP

Do not press.

Neck edging

With RS facing, work a row of dc evenly around neck edge and neckline edge, join with a ss to first dc. Fasten off. Join collar to neck edge. Join side and sleeve seam.

Using a beading needle, string pearl beads onto a matching thread. Couch thread in place between each pearl bead around cuffs, neckline and collar. Sew button to left side of front at neckline. Sew a buttonhole loop to right side of front opposite button.

BASKETWEAVE

Worked in a smooth, shiny mercerised cotton, this basketweave sweater with half sleeves can also be made into a sleeveless top. A bobbled edging and knitted ribbing trim the neckline and sleeves.

▶ **SIZES**
To fit 86[91:96]cm/34[36:38]in bust.
Note: Figures for larger sizes are in square brackets. If there is only one set of figures, it applies to all sizes.
See diagram for finished measurements.

▶ **MATERIALS** *See page 118 for further yarn information*
700[750:800]g (approx 185m per 50g) of a lightweight cotton yarn
4.50mm crochet hook *or size to obtain correct tension*
One pair of 3¾mm knitting needles

▶ **TENSION**
20 sts and 19 rows to 10cm over patt using 4.50mm hook.
Check your tension before beginning.

Note: When decreasing for neck, work one st dec by inserting hook around last 2 or first 2 htr of row, keeping edge st in dc. When increasing for sleeve, work one st inc by working 2 sts around first or last htr of row, keeping edge st in dc.

▶ **BACK**
Using hook, make 114[118:122]ch.
Base row 1htr into 3rd ch from hook, 1htr into each ch to end. Turn. 112[116:120]htr.
1st row (WS) 1ch, 1dc into first htr, yrh and insert hook from back to front and to back again around stem of next htr, yrh and draw a loop through, yrh and draw through all 3 loops on hook — called 1htr back —, 1htr back around each of next 0[2:4]htr, yrh and insert hook from front to back and to front again around stem of next htr, yrh and draw a loop through, yrh and draw through all 3 loops on hook — called 1htr front —, 1htr front around each of next 11htr, *1htr back around each of next 12htr, 1htr front around each of next 12htr, rep from *, ending with 1htr back around each of next 1[3:5]htr, 1dc into last htr. Turn. 112[116:120] sts.
2nd row (RS) 1ch, 1dc into first dc, 1htr front around each of next 1[3:5]htr, 1htr back around each of next 12htr, *1htr front around each of next 12htr, 1htr back around each of next 12htr, rep from *, ending with 1htr front around each of next 1[3:5]htr, 1dc into last dc. Turn.
3rd row 1ch, 1dc into first dc, 1htr back

around each of next 1[3:5]htr, 1htr front around each of next 12htr, *1htr back around each of next 12htr, 1htr front around each of next 12htr, rep from *, ending with 1htr back around each of next 1[3:5]htr, 1dc into last dc. Turn.
4th row 1ch, 1dc into first dc, 1htr front around each htr to last dc, 1dc into last dc. Turn.
5th row As 2nd row.
6th row As 3rd row.
7th row As 2nd row.
8th row As 4th row.
9th row As 3rd row.
Rep 2nd-9th rows to form patt. Cont in patt until back measures 33cm from beg, ending with a WS row.
Armhole shaping
Break off yarn and fasten off. Keeping patt correct and with RS facing, miss first 14[15:16] sts and rejoin yarn to top of next st with a ss, 1dc into same place as ss, work in patt to last 15[16:17] sts, 1dc into top of next st. Turn, leaving rem 14[15:16] sts unworked. 84[86:88] sts.
Work in patt without shaping until armhole measures 24[25:26]cm, ending with a WS row.
Shoulder and neck shaping
Break off yarn and fasten off. Keeping patt correct, and with RS facing, miss first 4[5:6] sts, rejoin yarn to top of next st with a ss, 1dc into same place as ss, work in patt over next 21htr, 1dc into top of next st, turn leaving rem 57[58:59] sts unworked. 23 sts.
Work first side of neck on these sts, dec one st at neck edge on next row (see

Note above) and on every foll row 3 times in all *and at the same time* dec 5 sts at armhole edge on every row 3 times in all. 5 sts. Fasten off.
With RS facing, miss centre 30 sts for centre back neck and rejoin yarn to top of next st with a ss, 1dc into same place as ss, work in patt over next 21htr, 1dc into top of next st, turn leaving rem 4[5:6] sts unworked. 23 sts.
Complete 2nd side of neck as for first side, reversing shaping.

▶ **FRONT**
Work as for back until armhole measures 17[18:19]cm, ending with a WS row.
Neck shaping
Keeping patt correct and with RS facing, work in patt across first 32[33:34] sts, 1dc into top of next st, turn leaving rem 51[52:53] sts unworked. 33[:34:35] sts.
Work first side of neck on these sts, dec one st at neck edge on next row and on every foll row 6 times in all, then on every alternate row 3 times. 24[25:26] sts.
Work without shaping until there are same number of rows as back to shoulder. Work shoulder shaping as for back.
With RS facing, miss 18 sts for centre front neck and rejoin yarn to top of next st with a ss, 1dc into same place as ss, work in patt over last 32[33:34] sts, turn. 33[34:35] sts.

The sleeveless variation still retains the bobbled neck edging and ribbing.

Complete 2nd side of neck as for first side, reversing shaping.

▶ **SLEEVES** (make 2)
Using hook, make 86[90:94]ch.
Work base row as for back. 84[88:92] sts.
1st row (WS) 1ch, 1dc into first htr, 1htr back around each of first 0[1:3]htr, 1htr front around each of next 11[12:12]htr, *1htr back around each of next 12htr, 1htr front around each of next 12htr, rep from *, ending last rep 1htr front around each of next 11[12:12]htr, 1htr back around each of next 0[1:3]htr, 1dc into last htr. Turn.
Cont in patt as set on back, inc one st at each end of every 5th row 6 times in all (see Note above), incorporating extra sts into patt. 96[100:104] sts.
Work without shaping until sleeve measures 24cm from beg. Fasten off.

▶ **BOBBLE EDGING**
Join left shoulder seam.
Using hook and with RS facing, beg at right shoulder and work 44dc evenly

along back neck, work 56dc evenly along front neck. 100dc.
Break off yarn and fasten off.
Using hook and with RS facing, rejoin yarn to first dc with a ss, 2ch, 1htr into same place as ss, 5htr into next dc, remove hook from loop and reinsert into top of first htr of 5htr group, then draw last loop through — called bobble —, *1htr into each of next 3dc, 1 bobble into next dc, rep from *, ending with 1htr into each of last 2dc. Fasten off.
Work 84dc along lower edge of sleeves and work bobble edging as for neck.

▶ **NECKBAND**
Using knitting needles and with RS facing, beg at right shoulder and pick up and K57 sts evenly along bobble edging of back neck, pick up and K66 sts evenly along front neck edge. 123 sts.
Work in K1, P1 rib (beg and ending first row with P1) for 6cm. Cast off loosely in rib.

▶ **CUFFS**
Using knitting needles and with RS facing, pick up and K105[111:117] sts evenly along bobble edging at lower edge of sleeve. Work rib as for neckband for 6cm. Cast off loosely in rib.

▶ **MAKING UP**
Press pieces very lightly on WS with a damp cloth and warm iron. Join right shoulder and neckband seam. Sew top of sleeve to vertical edge of armhole. Sew horizontal edge of armhole to side of sleeve. Join side and sleeve seams. Using hook and with RS facing, work 2 rounds of dc evenly along lower edge of back and front. Fasten off.

DESIGN VARIATION

▶ **SLEEVELESS TOP**
For sleeveless top omit sleeves. Work neckband as for version with sleeves. Join right shoulder seam and work 96[100:104]dc evenly along vertical edge of each armhole. Work bobble edging along these dc as for neck. Using knitting needles and with RS facing, pick up and K129[135:141] sts evenly along bobble edging. Work in rib as for neckband for 6cm. Cast off loosely in rib. Sew sides of ribbing to horizontal edges of armhole. Join side seams.

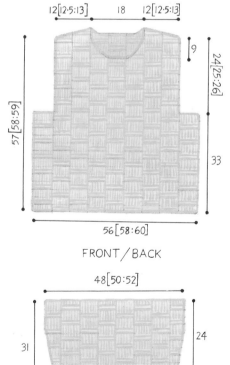

FRONT / BACK

SLEEVE

All measurements are in centimetres.

MOTIFS & PATTERNS

MOTIFS & PATTERNS

Colour patterns are probably the most neglected area of crochet, so creative crocheters would do well to apply their talents to charted designs — from pictorial to *trompe l'oeil* to motifs and Fair Isle type patterns. The samples shown here, which include only a few of the various types of charted colourwork motifs, patterns and colour stitches, give a hint of the hidden scope of simple crochet.

► FAIR ISLE CROCHET

Although Fair Isle is the technical term used for a specific type of knitting pattern originating in the Fair Isles of Scotland, the term has come to describe a particular type of design which is composed of detailed colour patterns worked alternately and repeated in stripes. Fair Isle denotes a delicacy rather than a boldness of pattern and colour. Used broadly it can be used to describe the colourwork on sample 5 or on *Bobbled Fair Isle* on page 90. The simple formula for composing original Fair Isle crochet designs is to make up three or more patterned stripes in contrasting colours, then combine and repeat these stripes.

► COLOUR STITCHES

Some crochet stitch patterns, which are constructed by combining different types of basic stitches, are worked in two or three colours. Elongated stitches (6, 7 and 8 — see page 70) and the diamond patterns (1 and 2) are examples of this method of colourwork. There are many other crochet colour stitch patterns, but these two types are interesting because of their flexibility. By working some of the diamonds or half diamonds in a contrasting colour, horizontal or vertical stripes, circles, large Argyll-type diamonds and triangles can be formed. Any of these would be attractive substitutes for *Diamonds* on page 80. Elongated stitches look striking worked in a yarn which contrasts in texture with the background. Samples 6, 7 and 8 have repeating motifs which are worked over nine stitches like the motif on *Fans* on page 72. They could therefore be used instead of the fans on the sweater.

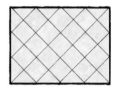

1 See page 80 for diamond stitch symbol chart. Work diamonds in colours as above.

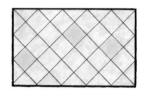

2 See page 80 for diamond stitch symbol chart. Using separate lengths of contrasting yarn, work random diamonds into a solid background as indicated here.

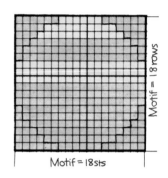

Motif = 18 rows

Motif = 18 sts

3 Tunisian crochet knit stitch.

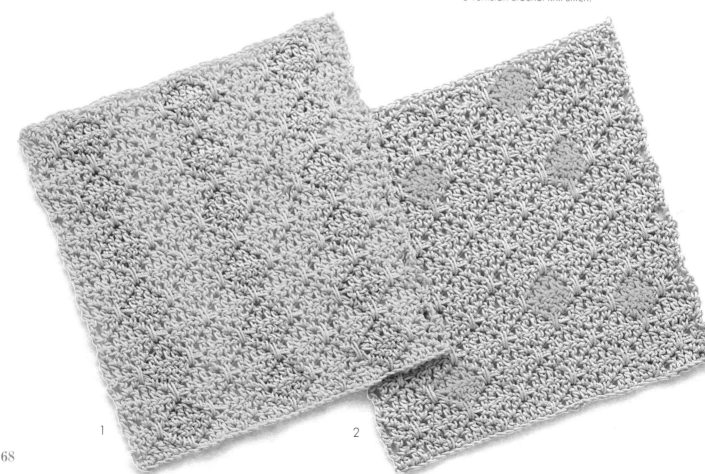

1

2

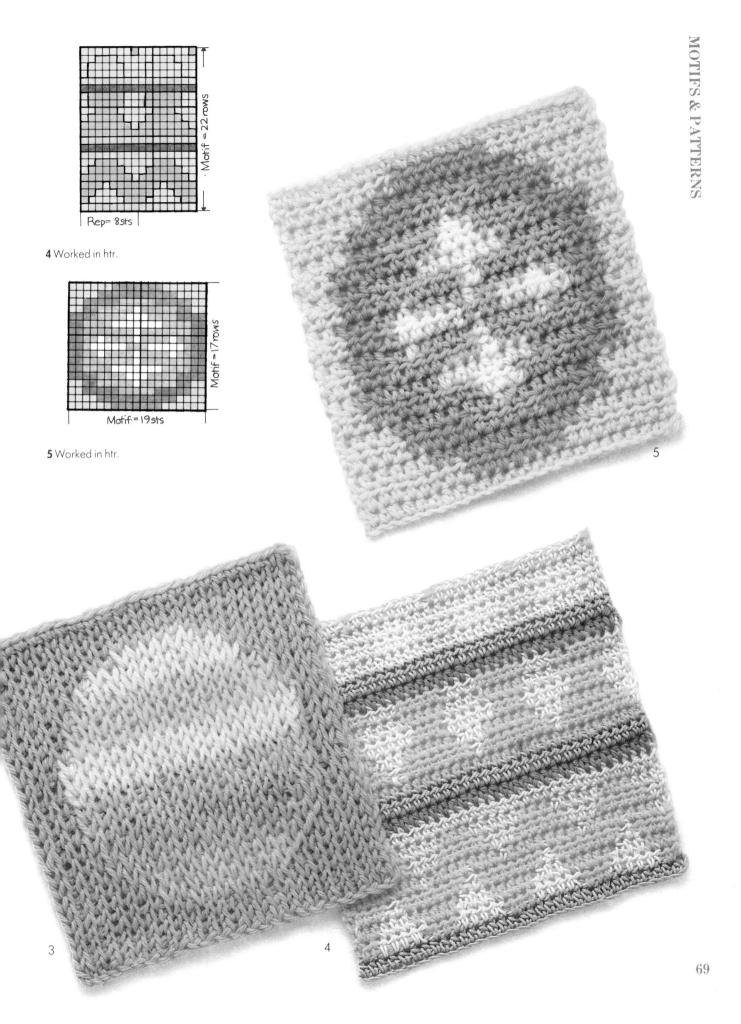

Rep= 8sts

4 Worked in htr.

Motif = 22 rows

Motif= 17 rows

Motif = 19 sts

5 Worked in htr.

5

3

4

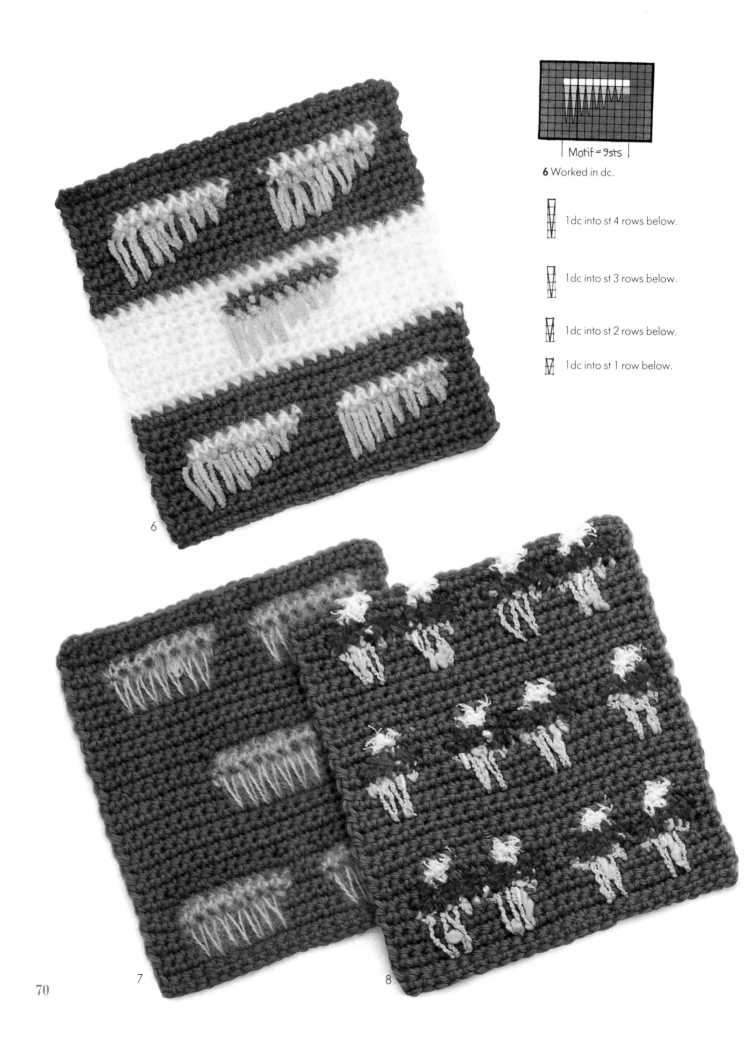

Motif = 9sts

6 Worked in dc.

1dc into st 4 rows below.

1dc into st 3 rows below.

1dc into st 2 rows below.

1dc into st 1 row below.

6

7

8

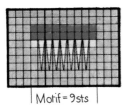

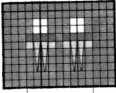

| Motif = 9sts |

7 Worked in dc.

| Motif = 9sts |

8 Worked in dc.

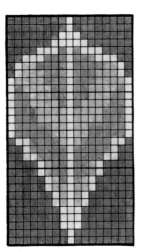

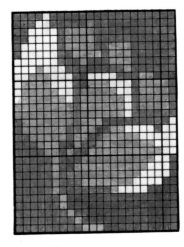

9 Worked in dc.

10 Worked in dc.

▶ **MOTIFS**

Charted motifs are fun to create with coloured pencils on graph paper. The motifs will not necessarily translate into crochet in the same shape as they appear on the graph paper. This depends on the crochet stitch used. The half treble stitch (3) is slightly longer than it is wide so the resulting motif will be more elongated than its graphed counterpart. But the individual stitches of Tunisian knit stitch (4) and double crochet (9 and 10) are roughly square. Sample 4 has exactly the same number of stitches across and rows in depth as *Winter flowers* on page 86. It would provide an interesting pastel alternative to the flower shape and would be easier to work. The motif of sample 3 could be sprinkled over *Colour blocks* on page 83 in place of the charted colour blocks or sample 9 or 10 could replace the double crochet leaf shape on *Leaves* on page 76. Charted garments are always easy to alter. All you need do is copy the chart outline, colour in an original design and work from the chart in the same yarns and tension as specified in the instructions.

9

10

FANS

Sprinkled with tiny fans, this chenille sweater is worked in a simple double crochet background with the motifs in elongated double crochet. The edgings on the crocheted cuffs and collar are knitted so that they roll back to give a neat finish.

▶ **SIZES**

To fit 81[86-91:96-102]cm/32[34-36: 38-40]in bust.

Note: Figures for larger sizes are in square brackets. If there is only one set of figures, it applies to all sizes. *See diagram for finished measurements.*

▶ **MATERIALS**

See page 118 for further yarn information
Use a lightweight cotton chenille (approx 145m per 50g), a shiny lightweight yarn (approx 115m per 50g) and a medium weight wool yarn (approx 115m per 50g):
450[500:600]g lightweight cotton chenille yarn in main colour MC (black)
200[200:250]g shiny lightweight yarn in contrasting colour A (cream)
50g medium weight wool yarn in B (black)
4.00mm crochet hook *or size to obtain correct tension*
One pair of 3¾mm knitting needles
3 buttons
Millinery wire for collar (optional)

▶ **TENSION**

12 sts to 7cm and 20 rows to 10cm over fan patt using 4.00mm hook.
Check your tension before beginning (see Note below).

Note: To check tension make 28ch and work base row as for back. 27dc.

Work 6 rows in dc, then beg fan patt as for *1st patt row* of back, foll instructions for largest size. Work at least 18 rows in fan patt before measuring tension. Make sure that elongated dc sts are worked *loosely* so that they do not pull tog the fabric. When working with 2 colours in a row, carry colour not in use across the top of previous row and work all sts over it (see page 112).

▶ **BACK**

Using hook and MC, make 94[96: 100]ch.
Base row 1dc into 2nd ch from hook, 1dc into each ch to end. Turn. 93[95:99]dc.

1st row 1ch, 1dc into each dc to end. Turn.
Rep last row 3[5:7] times more.
Beg fan patt as foll:
1st patt row (RS) 1ch, 1dc into each of next 0[1:3]dc changing to A with last yrh of last st, *(work fan over next 9dc as foll) using A, 1dc in next dc, miss next 7dc and work next 7 sts into rows below, insert hook from front to back through top of dc one row below next st, yrh and draw a loop through pulling loop up to height of previous row so that fabric is not pulled tog, yrh and draw through 2 loops on hook — called 1dc into next dc one row below —, 1dc into next dc 2 rows below, 1dc into each of next 3dc 3 rows below, 1dc into next dc 2 rows below, 1dc into next dc 1 row below, 1dc into next dc in previous row changing to MC with last yrh of last dc — called 1 fan —, using MC, 1dc into each of next 3dc changing to A with last yrh of last dc, rep from *, ending last rep with 0[1:3]dc in MC. Turn.
2nd row 1ch, using MC, 1dc into each of next 0[1:3]dc changing to A with last yrh of last st, *using A, 1dc into each of next 9dc of fan changing to MC with

last yrh of last dc, using MC, 1dc into each of next 3dc changing to A with last yrh of last dc, rep from *, ending last rep with 0[1:3]dc in MC. Turn.
3rd-14th rows Using MC, 1ch, 1dc into each dc to end. Turn.
15th row 1ch, 1dc into each of next 6[7:9]dc, *1 fan in A, using MC, 1dc into each of next 3dc, rep from *, ending last rep with 6[7:9]dc in MC. Turn.
16th row 1ch, using MC, 1dc into each of next 6[7:9]dc changing to A with last yrh of last st, *using A, 1dc into each of next 9dc of fan changing to MC with last yrh of last dc, using MC, 1dc into each of next 3dc changing to A with

last yrh of last dc, rep from *, ending last rep with 6[7:9]dc in MC. Turn.

17th-28th rows As 3rd-14th rows.
Last 28 rows form fan patt and are rep throughout.
Cont in fan patt until 7 rows of fans have been completed from beg, ending with a 2nd patt row.
Work 4 rows in dc, using MC only. Fasten off.

Neck and shoulder shaping
Next row Using hook and MC and with RS facing, miss first 9[9:10]dc and rejoin yarn to next dc with a ss, 1ch, 1dc into same place as ss, 1dc into each of next 28dc. Turn, leaving rem sts unworked.

Next row 1ch, (insert hook into next dc, yrh and draw a loop through) twice, yrh and draw through all 3 loops on hook — called 2dc tog —, 1dc into each of next 18dc. Turn, leaving rem sts unworked.

Next row Ss over first 9dc, 1dc into each of next 8dc, 2dc tog. Fasten off.
With RS facing, miss centre 17[19:21]dc, rejoin MC to next st and work 2nd shoulder in the same way reversing shaping.

▶ **FRONT**
Using hook and MC, make 94[96: 100]ch. Work base and first row as for back. 93[95:99]dc.
Work 3[5:7] rows more in dc.
Beg fan patt as foll:
1st patt row As for 15th patt row of back.
2nd patt row As for 16th patt row of back.
3rd-14th rows As for 3rd-14th rows of back.

15th row As for first row of back.

16th row As for 2nd row of back.

17th-28th rows As for 3rd-14th rows of back.

Last 28 rows form fan patt and are rep throughout.

Cont in fan patt until 5 rows of fans have been completed from beg, ending with a 2nd patt row.

Work one row in dc, using MC only.

Neck slit

Next row (WS) Using MC, 1ch, 1dc into each dc to centre dc. Turn, leaving rem 47[48:50]dc unworked.

Keeping to fan patt as set, cont on these 46[47:49]dc until one more row of fans has been completed, omitting first fan at neck edge and ending with a WS row.

Work 10 rows more in dc, using MC only. Fasten off.

Neck shaping

Next row (RS) Using hook and MC and with RS facing, miss first 5[6:7]dc at neck edge and rejoin yarn to next dc with a ss, 1ch, 1dc into same place as ss, 1dc into each dc to end. Turn.

Cont in fan patt, dec one st at neck edge on next 5 rows. 36[36:37]dc. Work in fan patt without shaping until front has same number of rows as back to shoulder shaping, so ending at neck edge.

Shoulder shaping

Next row (RS) Using MC, 1ch, 1dc into each of first 27dc. Turn, leaving rem 9[9:10]dc unworked.

Next row Ss over first 9 dc, 1dc into each dc to end. Turn.

Next row 1ch, 1dc into each of first 9dc.

Fasten off.

Using hook and MC and with WS facing, miss centre st and rejoin yarn to next dc with a ss, 1ch, 1dc into same place as ss, 1dc into each dc to end. Complete 2nd side of neck in the same way, reversing shaping.

▶ **RIGHT SLEEVE**

Right side of sleeve

Using hook and MC, make 29[29:30]ch. Work base and first rows as for back. 28[28:29]dc.

2nd row (WS) Work in dc, inc 4[6:6] sts evenly across row. Turn. 32[34:35]dc.

Work 3 rows in dc without shaping.

6th row (WS) Work in dc, inc one st at end of row (side edge). Turn.

Cont in dc, inc one st at side edge on every 3rd row twice. 35[37:38]dc. Work 2 rows without shaping, so ending with a WS row. Do not break off yarn. Set aside right side of sleeve.

Left side of sleeve

Using hook and MC, make 11[11:12]ch. Work base and first rows as for right side of sleeve. 10[10:11]dc.

2nd row (WS) Work in dc, inc 2 sts evenly across row. Turn. 12[12:13]dc.

Work 3 rows in dc without shaping.

6th row Work in dc, inc one st at beg of row (side edge).

Work as for right side of sleeve from ** to **. 15[15:16]dc. Fasten off.

Join sleeve

Join right and left sides of sleeve as foll:

Next row With RS facing, cont on right side of sleeve, 1ch, 2dc into first dc, work in dc to end, 1ch, cont in dc across left side of sleeve to last dc, 2dc into last dc. Turn.

Next row 1ch, 1dc into each dc to 1ch, 1dc into 1ch, 1dc into each dc to end. Turn. 53[55:57]dc.

Work one row without shaping.

Inc one st at each end of next row. 55[57:59]dc.

Beg fan patt as foll:

Next row (RS) Using MC, 1ch, 1dc into each of first 5[6:7]dc, *1 fan in A, using MC, 1dc into each of next 3dc, rep from *, ending last rep with 5[6:7]dc in MC. Turn.

Cont in fan patt as set for back *and at the same time* shape sleeve by inc one

st at each end of every 3rd row 0[4:8] times, then every 4th row 12[9:6] times (counting from last inc row), adding fans as sleeve widens. 79[83:87]dc.

Work 2[3:4] rows without shaping. Fasten off.

▶ **LEFT SLEEVE**

Left side of sleeve

Using hook and MC, make 29[29:30]ch.

Work base-5th rows as for right side of right sleeve. 32[34:35]dc.

6th row (WS) Work in dc, inc one st at beg of row (side edge). Turn.

Work as for right side of right sleeve from ** to **. Fasten off.

Set left side of sleeve aside.

Right side of sleeve

Using hook and MC, make 11[11:12]ch.

Work base-5th rows as for left side of right sleeve. 12[12:13]dc.

6th row (WS) Work in dc, inc one st at end of row (side edge). Turn.

Work as for right side of right sleeve from ** to **. 15[15:16]dc.

Do not break off yarn.

Join sleeve

Join right and left sides and complete as for right sleeve.

▶ **COLLAR**

Sew shoulder seams.

Note: When working stripe rib patt, carry colour not in use *loosely* across top of previous row, working all sts over it. To ensure that carried yarn does not shorten width of row pull collar gently widthwise at end of each row.

Using hook and MC, make 15ch. Work base row as for back. 14dc.

**Beg stripe rib patt as foll:

1st row (RS) Using A, 1ch, working into *back* loops only, 1dc into each dc to end. Turn.

2nd row (RS) Using MC, 1ch, working

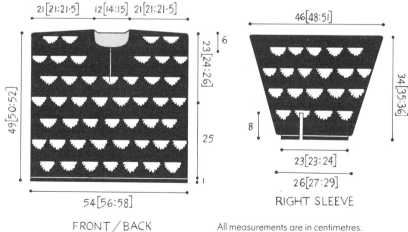

FRONT / BACK

All measurements are in centimetres.

RIGHT SLEEVE

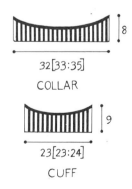

COLLAR

CUFF

into back loops only, 1dc into each dc to last 2dc, 2dc tog. Turn.
Rep last 2 rows 3 times more. 10dc.
Work 3 rows in stripe rib patt without shaping. Rep 2nd row.** 9dc.
Work 3 rows without shaping. Mark last row. Rep 2nd row.
Cont in stripe rib patt on these 8dc until collar fits from centre front to centre back, placing *shaped edge* of collar along neck edge, ending with a stripe in A. Mark last row as centre back.
Cont in stripe rib patt, work same number of rows as between 2 markers, so ending with a row in MC at shaped edge.
Next row Using A, 1ch, 2dc into first dc, work in patt to end. Turn. 9dc.
Cont in stripe rib patt, inc one st at beg of every 4th row twice, then at beg of every other row 3 times. 14dc.
Work one row without shaping.
Fasten off.

▶ **CUFFS** (make 2)
Using hook and MC, make 16ch.
Work base row as for back. 15dc.
Work as for collar from ** to **. 10dc.
Mark last row in A.
Cont in stripe rib patt until cuff measures 11[11:12]cm from beg, ending with a stripe in A. Mark last row as centre of cuff.
Cont in stripe rib patt, work same number of rows as between 2 markers, so ending with a row in MC at shaped edge.
Next row Using A, 1ch, 2dc into first

dc, work in patt to end. Turn. 11dc.
Cont in stripe rib patt, inc one st at beg of 4th row, then at beg of every other row 3 times. 15dc.
Work one row without shaping.
Fasten off.

▶ **KNITTED ROLLED EDGINGS**
Back edging
Using knitting needles and B and with RS facing, pick up and K7 sts for every 5 foundation ch along lower edge of back (see page 115).
Knit one row. Purl one row.
Rep from * to * once more.
Cast off tightly in knit.
Front edging
Work as for back edging.
Collar edging
Using knitting needles and B and with RS facing, pick up and K3 sts for every 2 row ends all along *straight* edge of collar. Complete edging as for back edging.
Cuff edgings
Work as for collar edging, but pick up sts along *shaped* edge.

▶ **MAKING UP**
Do not press. Mark positions for sleeves on back and front 23[24:26]cm from shoulder seams. Sew sleeves between markers. Join sleeve and side seams.
Darn in all loose ends.
Sew on collar with RS of shaped edge of collar facing WS of neck edge and neck edge slightly overlapping collar.

Neck edging
Using hook and B and with RS facing work a row of dc evenly along short edge of collar, beg at left side of collar and working into folded rolled edge and then into sps between dc (not into foundation ch), cont in dc around slit edge (working 2dc into end of slit) and along short end of right side of collar. Fasten off.
With RS facing, rejoin B to beg of last row and work a 2nd row in ss, inserting hook through both loops of top of each dc of previous row. Fasten off.
If desired, insert length of millinery wire through edging at short edges of collar to stiffen. Bend ends at WS and secure in place with B.
Sew button in place on left side of neck slit and work a ch for button loop on opposite side.
Cuff and sleeve slit edging
Using hook and B, work a row of dc evenly along sleeve slit, working 2dc into end of slit. Using hook and B, work a row of dc evenly along short ends of cuff. Fasten off. Work a 2nd row in ss as for neck edging.
Pin cuff to sleeve with WS of cuff facing RS of sleeve.
Using hook and B, work 39[39:41]dc evenly along sleeve edge, working through cuff and foundation ch of sleeve with each dc. Fasten off.
Sew a button to each sleeve slit and work button loop opposite as for neck.

LEAVES

Slubbed cotton yarn in double crochet produces a firm fabric for this colourful T-shaped top. This design can be varied by making a slipover top without the sleeves, designing your own motifs or leaving the motifs off.

▶ SIZES
To fit 81[86:91:96-102]cm/32[34:36: 38-40]in bust.
Note: Figures for larger sizes are in square brackets. If there is only one set of figures, it applies to all sizes.
See diagram for finished measurements.

▶ MATERIALS
See page 118 for further yarn information
Use a medium weight slubbed cotton yarn (approx 100m per 50g):
500[500:550:550]g in main colour MC (yellow)
150g in contrasting colour A (turquoise)
150[200:200:250]g in contrasting colour B (white)
5.00mm crochet hook *or size to obtain correct tension*
One pair of 4mm knitting needles

▶ TENSION
16dc and 20 rows to 10cm over patt using 5.00mm hook.
Check your tension before beginning.

Note: When working leaves, do not carry colours across back of work, but use a separate bobbin of yarn for each block of colour (see page 112). When working from chart, read odd-numbered rows from right to left and even-numbered rows from left to right. Always change to new colour with last yrh of previous st.

▶ BACK
Using hook and MC, make 85[89: 93:97]ch.
Base row 1dc into 2nd ch from hook, 1dc into each ch to end. Turn. 84[88:92:96]dc.
1st row 1ch, 1dc into each dc to end. Turn.
Work 0[0:2:2] rows in dc. Cont in dc foll chart, beg with 3rd[1st:1st:1st] row of chart.**
When 113th row of chart has been completed, work neck shaping as foll:
Neck shaping
Next row (WS) Work first 24[26:28:30] sts in patt. Turn, leaving rem sts unworked.
Dec one st at neck edge on next row and then at neck edge on every foll row 3 times in all. 21[23:25:27]dc.
Work one row without shaping. Fasten off.

With WS facing, return to rem sts, miss next 36dc for centre back neck, rejoin MC to rem sts and work in patt to end. Work 2nd side of neck to match first side, reversing shaping. Fasten off.

▶ FRONT
Work as for back to **. When 102nd row of chart has been completed, work neck shaping as foll:
Neck shaping
Next row (RS) Work first 29[31:33:35]

sts in patt. Turn, leaving rem sts unworked.
Dec 2 sts at neck edge on next 2 rows, then one st at neck edge on next row and 3 foll alternate rows. 21[23:25:27]dc.
Cont without shaping until front measures same as back to shoulder. Fasten off.
With RS facing, return to rem sts, miss next 26dc for centre front neck, rejoin MC to rem sts and work in patt to end. Complete to match first side, reversing shaping.

▶ SLEEVES (make 2)
Using hook and MC, make 61[65: 69:69]ch. Work base and first rows as for back. 60[64:68:68]dc.
Cont in dc foll chart for sleeve, beg with first row of chart and inc one st at each end of 7th row and then every foll 8th row until there are 66[70:74:74] sts. When 30th row of chart has been completed, work without shaping until sleeve measures 17cm from beg or desired sleeve length. Fasten off.

▶ BACK RIB
Using knitting needles and MC and with RS facing, pick up and K108[112:116:120] sts evenly along lower edge of back (see page 115). Beg rib as foll:
1st rib row *K2, P2, rep from * to end. Last row forms rib patt. Cont until rib measures 2.5cm. Cast off loosely in rib.

▶ FRONT RIB
Work as for back rib.

▶ SLEEVE EDGING
Using knitting needles and MC and with RS facing, pick up and K60[64:68:68] sts evenly along lower edge of sleeve. Work for 2.5cm in K2, P2 rib as for back rib.

▶ **NECKBAND**
Join right shoulder seam. Using knitting needles and MC and with RS facing, pick up and K132 sts evenly around neck edge. Work for 2.5cm in K2, P2 rib as for back rib.

▶ **MAKING UP**
Darn in all loose ends. Join left shoulder and neckband seam. Mark positions for sleeves on back and front 21[22:23:23]cm from shoulder seam. Sew on sleeves between markers. Join sleeve and side seams. Press seams lightly on WS with warm iron.

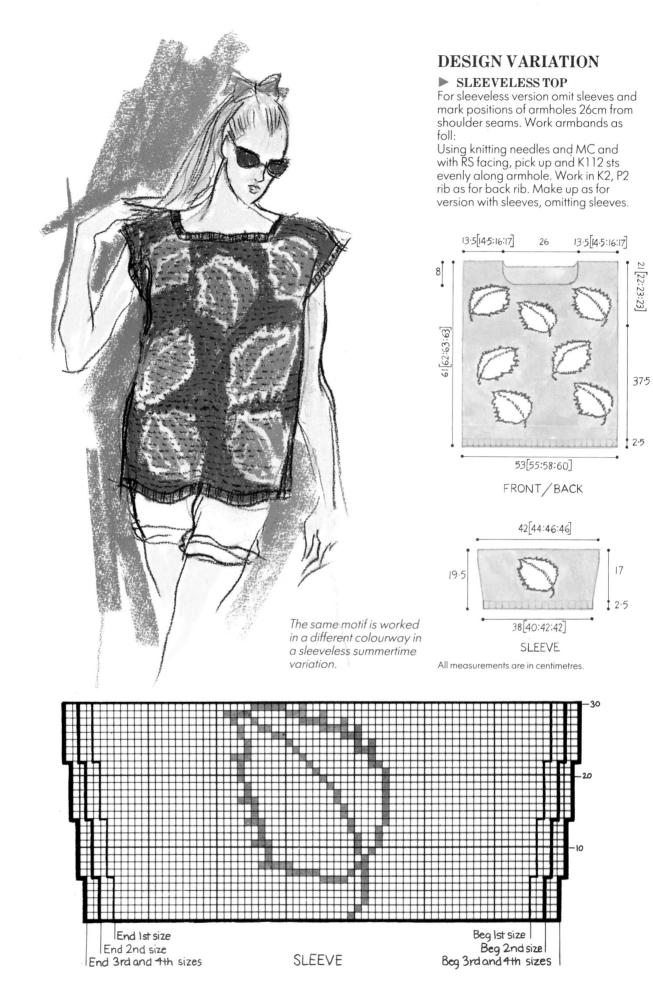

DESIGN VARIATION

▶ SLEEVELESS TOP

For sleeveless version omit sleeves and mark positions of armholes 26cm from shoulder seams. Work armbands as foll:

Using knitting needles and MC and with RS facing, pick up and K112 sts evenly along armhole. Work in K2, P2 rib as for back rib. Make up as for version with sleeves, omitting sleeves.

13·5[14·5:16:17]   26   13·5[14·5:16:17]

8   21[22:23:23]

61[62:63:63]   37·5

2·5

53[55:58:60]

FRONT / BACK

42[44:46:46]

19·5   17

2·5

38[40:42:42]

SLEEVE

All measurements are in centimetres.

The same motif is worked in a different colourway in a sleeveless summertime variation.

30

20

10

End 1st size
End 2nd size
End 3rd and 4th sizes

SLEEVE

Beg 1st size
Beg 2nd size
Beg 3rd and 4th sizes

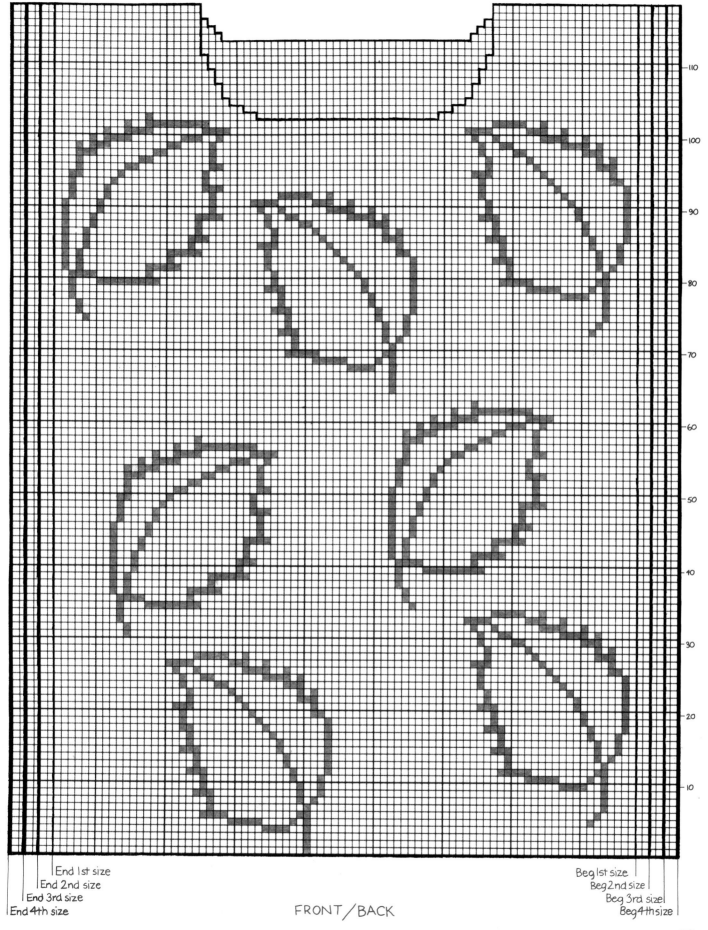

FRONT / BACK

DIAMONDS

Varying the heights of the stitches in each row creates the diamond shapes in this design so that you are only working with one colour and one ball of yarn at a time. For a cooler and more youthful top, work the cropped version on page 82.

▶ **SIZES**
To fit 81-86[91-96]cm/32-34[36-38]in bust.
Note: Figures for larger size are in square brackets. If there is only one set of figures, it applies to both sizes. *See diagram for finished measurements.*

▶ **MATERIALS**
See page 118 for further yarn information
Use a lightweight cotton yarn (approx 185m per 50g):
175[225]g in each of 2 colours A (green) and B (pale blue)
25g in C (turquoise)
3.00mm crochet hook *or size to obtain correct tension*
4 buttons

▶ **TENSION**
22 sts and 17 rows to 10cm over diamond patt using 3.00mm hook. *Check your tension before beginning (see Note below).*

Note: To check tension make 32ch and work base-5th rows of back or foll symbol chart. Cont in patt until sample measures 12cm. Before measuring tension, block swatch using damp cloth and warm iron.

▶ **BACK**
Using A, make 104[116]ch.
Base row 1dc into 2nd ch from hook, *1htr into next ch, 1tr into next ch, 1dtr into next ch, 1tr into next ch, 1htr into next ch, 1dc into next ch, rep from * to end. Turn. 103[115]sts.
1st row Using B, 3ch, miss first dc, *1tr into next st, 1htr into next st, 1ch, miss

next st (dtr), 1htr into next st, 1tr into next st, 1dtr into next st, rep from * to end. Turn. 103[115] sts, counting first 3ch as first st.
2nd row Using B, 3ch, miss first dtr, *1tr into next st, 1htr into next st, 1dc into top of dtr missed in last row working over 1ch worked in last row, 1htr into next st, 1tr into next st, 1dtr into next st, rep from *, working last dtr into 3rd of 3ch. Turn.
3rd row Using A, 1ch, 1dc into first st, *1htr into next st, 1tr into next st, 1dtr into top of dtr 2 rows below (into same place as dc in last row), 1tr into next st, 1htr into next st, 1ch, miss next st (dtr), rep from *, omitting 1ch at end of last rep and working 1dc into 3rd of 3ch. Turn.
4th row Using A, 1ch, 1dc into first st, *1htr into next st, 1tr into next st, 1dtr into next st, 1tr into next st, 1htr into next st, 1dc into top of dtr missed in last row, rep from *, working last dc into dc at end of row. Turn.
5th row Using B, 3ch, miss first dc, *1tr into next st, 1htr into next st, 1ch, miss next st (dtr), 1htr into next st, 1tr into next st, 1dtr into top of dtr 2 rows below (into same place as dc in last row), rep from *, working last dtr into dc at end of row. Turn.
Rep 2nd-5th rows to form diamond patt. **Cont in patt until 34[38] rows have been worked from beg counting base row, so ending with a 5th patt row.

Armhole shaping
Next row Using B, 1ch, 1ss into each of first 3 sts, 1dc into top of dtr missed in last row, rep from * of 4th row to last 3 sts. Turn, leaving last 3 sts unworked. 97[109] sts.
Next row Using A, as 5th row.
Next row Using A, as 2nd row.
Next row Using B, as 3rd row.
Next row Using B, as 4th row.
Cont in patt as now set until 34 rows have been worked from beg of armhole, so ending with a 5th patt row in A.

Neck shaping
Next row Using A, 3ch, miss first dtr, rep from * of 2nd row 4[5] times, 1tr

into next st, 1htr into next st, 1dc into top of dtr missed in last row. Turn, leaving rem sts unworked. 4[5] diamonds. Fasten off A.
Next row Miss first 3 sts and rejoin B to first dtr of last row with a ss, 1ch, 1dc into same dtr, rep from * of 3rd row to end. Turn.
Next row Using B, as 4th row.
Next row Using A, as 5th row. Fasten off.
Work 2nd side of neck as for first side, reversing shaping.

▶ **LEFT FRONT**
Using A, make 56[62]ch and work base and first rows as for back. Turn. 55[61] sts. Cont in patt as for back until left front has same number of rows as back to armhole.
Armhole shaping
Next row Using B, 1ch, ss into each of first 3 sts, 1dc into top of dtr missed in last row, rep from * of 4th row of back to last 3 sts, 1htr into next st, 1tr into next st, 1dtr into last st. Turn. 52[58] sts.
Next row Using A, 1ch, 1dc into first st, rep from * of 3rd row of back to last 3 sts, 1htr into next st, 1tr into next st, 1dtr into last st. Turn.
Next row Using A, 3ch, miss first dtr, rep from * of 2nd row of back to last 3 sts, 1tr into next st, 1htr into next st, 1dc into last st. Turn.
Next row Using B, 3ch, miss first dc, rep from * of 5th row of back to last 3 sts, 1htr into next st, 1tr into next st, 1dtr into last st. Turn.
Next row Using B, 1ch, 1dc into first st, rep from * of 4th row of back to last 3 sts, 1htr into next st, 1tr into next st, 1dtr into last st. Turn.
Rep last 4 rows to form diamond patt. Cont in patt until 24[20] rows have been worked from beg of armhole, so ending in the middle of a row of diamonds in B.
Neck shaping
Next row Using B, 1ch, 1dc into first st, rep from * of 4th row of back over first 5[6] diamonds. Turn, leaving rem sts unworked. 5[6] diamonds. Fasten off B.
Next row Miss first 3 sts and rejoin A to first dtr of last row with a ss, 1dc into same dtr, 1htr into next st, 1tr into next st, 1dtr into top of dtr 2 rows below, rep from * of 5th row of back to end. Turn.
Next row Using A, 3ch, miss first dtr, 1tr into next st, 1htr into next st, 1dc into top of dtr missed in last row, rep from * of 4th row of back to end. Turn. Fasten off A.
Next row Miss first 3 sts and rejoin B to first dtr of last row with a ss, 1ch, 1dc into same dtr, rep from * of 3rd row of back to end. Turn. 4[5] diamonds.
Cont in patt until left front has same number of rows as back to shoulder. Fasten off.

Foundation ch = multiple of 6ch plus 2 extra.

✳ In 3rd and 5th rows work dtr into top of dtr 2 rows below.

⊕ 1dc into dtr missed in row below. (See page 117 for other crochet symbols).

▶ RIGHT FRONT

Work as for left front until 6 rows have been worked from beg counting base row, so ending with 5th patt row. Set aside right front and using a separate length of B, make 5ch and fasten off. Cont on right front as foll:

Next row Using B, 3ch, miss first dtr, 1tr into next st, 1htr into next st, 1dc into top of dtr missed in last row, pick up separate ch in B and work 1htr into first ch, 1tr into next ch, 1dtr into next ch, 1tr into next ch, 1htr into last ch, miss 5 sts of last row and work 1dc into top of next dtr missed in last row, work in patt to end. Turn.

Work 15 rows in patt, then rep buttonhole row and cont in this way working a buttonhole on every 16th row until there are 4 buttonholes *and*

at the same time work as for left front, reversing armhole and neck shaping.

▶ MAKING UP

Darn in all loose ends. Press pieces on WS with a damp cloth and a warm iron, blocking to correct measurements. Join shoulder and side seams.

Edging

Using B and with RS facing, work a row of dc evenly up right front around neck and down left front, working 3dc at corners. Using C and with RS facing, beg at right side seam and work a row of dc evenly along lower edge of right front (working 2dc for every 3 foundation ch), cont in dc up right front, around neck, down left front and around lower edge of left front and

back as for lower edge of right front, working 3dc into corners. Join with a ss to first dc, turn, 1ch, insert hook from front to back and to front again around first dc, yrh and draw through both loops on hook — called dc around stem (see page 110)—, cont around edging working 1dc around stem of each dc and 2dc around stem of st at each corner. Join with a ss to first dc of row and fasten off.

Using B and with RS facing, work a row of dc evenly around armhole edge. Change to C and join with a ss to first st, 1ch, 1dc into each dc to end, join with a ss to first dc, turn, 1ch, 1dc around stem of each dc, join with a ss to first dc. Fasten off.

Press seams and edging on WS with a damp cloth and a warm iron. Sew on buttons opposite buttonholes.

DESIGN VARIATION

▶ CROPPED TOP

For a cropped top work back to **, then cont in patt until 18[22] rows have been worked from beg counting base row, so ending with a 5th patt row. Work armhole shaping and complete back as for longer version. Work left and right fronts foll instructions, but working 3 buttonholes instead of 4. Make up as for longer version.

A cooler, midriff top is produced by shortening the design and altering the colourway.

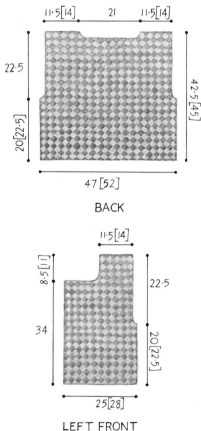

BACK

LEFT FRONT

All measurements are in centimetres.

COLOUR BLOCKS

Perfect for using leftover yarns, this charted sweater is worked in half trebles using smooth yarns and mohair. Follow the chart or create your own design after copying the outline onto graph paper, drawing in shapes and colouring them with crayons to see the final effect.

▶ **SIZES**
To fit 81[86-91:96-102]cm/32[34-36: 38-40]in bust.
Note: Figures for larger sizes are in square brackets. If there is only one set of figures, it applies to all sizes.
See diagram for finished measurements.

▶ **MATERIALS**
See page 118 for further yarn information
Use a lightweight wool yarn (approx 67m per 25g) and a lightweight mohair (approx 155m per 50g):
50[50:75]g lightweight wool yarn in each of 4 colours A (yellow), B (coral), C (beige) and D (pale pink)
50g lightweight wool yarn in each of 3 colours E (orange), F (pink) and H (pale yellow)

25g lightweight wool yarn in each of 2 colours I (dusty rose) and G (pale orange)
100[100:150]g lightweight mohair J (light green)
5.00mm and 5.50mm crochet hooks *or sizes to obtain correct tensions*

▶ TENSION

15htr and 13 rows to 10cm over colour patt using 5.00mm hook.
15dc and 14 rows to 10cm over rib patt using J and 5.50mm hook.
Check your tensions before beginning.

Note: Use a separate bobbin of yarn for each block of colour. When changing colours, change to new colour with last yrh of previous htr keeping yarn on WS (see page 112) Read odd-numbered chart rows (RS) from right to left and even-numbered rows from left to right.

▶ BACK

Using smaller hook and A, make 66[68:70]ch, then change to B and make 16[18:20]ch.
Base row (WS) Using B, 1htr into 3rd ch from hook, 1htr into each of next 12[14:16]ch changing to A with last yrh of last st, using A 1htr into each ch to end. Turn. 80[84:88]htr.
1st row (RS) Using A, 2ch, 1htr into each of first 67[69:71]htr, using B 1htr into each htr to end. Turn.
Foll chart for colour patt and beg with 2nd chart row, cont in htr as for last row until 35th chart row has been completed.
Armhole shaping
Next row (36th chart row) Work over first 2 sts in ss, 2ch, work in patt to last 2 sts. Turn, leaving rem 2 sts unworked. 76[80:84]htr.
Cont armhole shaping foll chart and working single decs at beg of row as

foll: 2ch, yrh and insert hook into first htr, yrh and draw a loop through, yrh and insert hook into next htr, yrh and draw a loop through, yrh and draw through all 5 loops on hook — called 2htr tog. Work decs at end of row by working 2htr tog over last 2 sts. When armhole shaping has been completed, work without shaping on rem 70[72:74]htr foll chart until 68th[70th:72nd] chart row has been completed. Work neck and shoulder shaping as indicated. Fasten off.

▶ FRONT

Work as for back until 60th chart row has been completed. Work neck and then shoulder shaping as indicated. Fasten off.

▶ COLLAR

Sew shoulder seams.
Using larger hook and J, make 11ch.
Base row 1dc into 2nd ch from hook, 1dc into each ch to end. Turn. 10dc.
1st row 1ch, working into *back* loops only, work 1dc into each dc to end. Turn.
Last row forms rib patt and is rep throughout. Cont in rib patt until collar, slightly stretched, fits around neck edge. Fasten off.

▶ BACK RIB

Using larger hook and J, make 6ch and work base and first rows as for collar. 5dc. Cont in rib patt until rib fits across lower edge of back. Fasten off.

▶ FRONT RIB

Work as for back rib.

▶ ARMHOLE BANDS (make 2)

Using larger hook and J, make 6ch and work base and first rows as for collar. 5dc. Cont in rib patt until band, slightly stretched, fits around armhole. Fasten off.

DESIGN VARIATION

▶ TOP WITHOUT RIBBING

For a simpler version of the sleeveless top omit crochet ribs, so that armholes and neck are edged with a single row of dc only.

▶ MAKING UP

Do not press. Darn in all loose ends. Using smaller hook and matching colours, work a row of dc evenly around neck edge and armhole. Sew armhole bands to armholes. Sew on front and back ribs. Join side seams. Join collar seam and sew collar in place to neck edge, lining collar seam up with left shoulder seam.

Removing the ribbing and using a different colourway produces a simple variation.

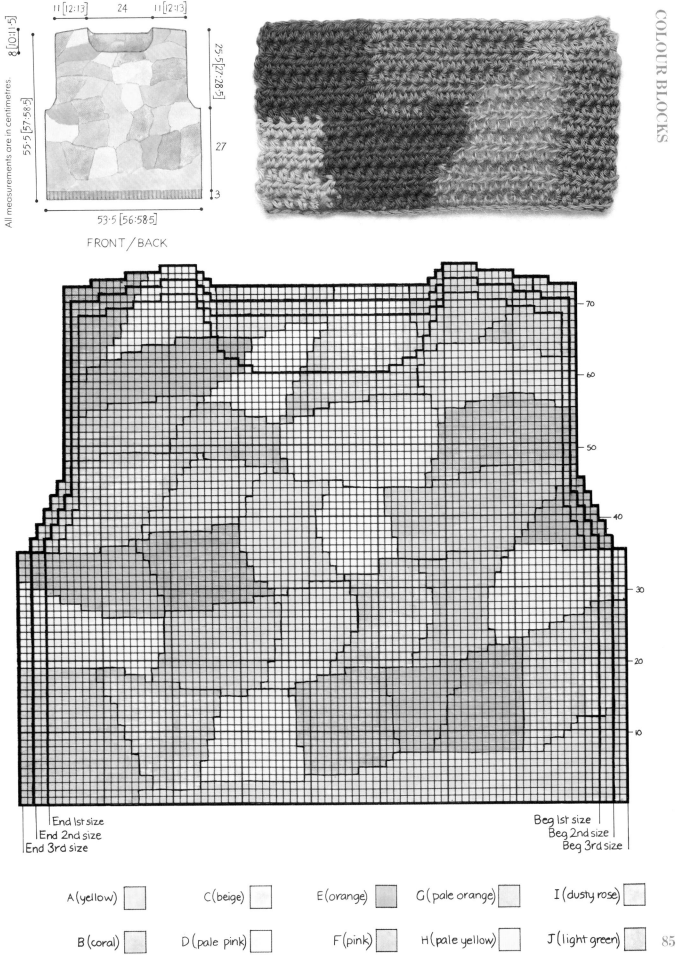

All measurements are in centimetres.

11 [12:13]   24   11 [12:13]

8 [10:11·5]

55·5 [57:58·5]

25·5 [27:28·5]

27

3

53·5 [56:58·5]

FRONT / BACK

70

60

50

40

30

20

10

End 1st size
End 2nd size
End 3rd size

Beg 1st size
Beg 2nd size
Beg 3rd size

A (yellow)

C (beige)

E (orange)

G (pale orange)

I (dusty rose)

B (coral)

D (pale pink)

F (pink)

H (pale yellow)

J (light green)

85

WINTER FLOWERS

Hardly distinguishable from knitted stocking stitch, Tunisian crochet knit stitch produces a warm fabric. With front pockets, long sleeves and a stand-up collar, this jacket is worked in panels using a simple charted motif and sewn together afterwards.

▶ **SIZES**

To fit 81[86:91]cm/32[34:36]in bust.
Note: Figures for larger sizes are in square brackets. If there is only one set of figures, it applies to all sizes.
See diagram for finished measurements.

▶ **MATERIALS**

See page 118 for further yarn information
Use a lightweight wool yarn (approx 67m per 25g):
200[250:300]g in A (beige)
125g in B (blue)

375[425:500]g in C (grey)
100g in D (white)
6.00mm Tunisian crochet hook *or size to obtain correct tension*
4.00mm crochet hook
Hooks and eyes for fastening
Shoulder pads (optional)

▶ TENSION

17 sts and 20 loop rows to 10cm over Tunisian crochet knit st worked in one colour only and using 6.00mm Tunisian hook.

17 sts and 18 loop rows to 10cm over Tunisian crochet knit st worked in colour patt using 6.00mm Tunisian hook.
24 sts and 24 rows to 10cm over seed patt using 4.00mm crochet hook.
Check your tensions before beginning.

Note: Back, fronts and sleeves are made in panels which are sewn tog. When working with 2 colours in a row, strand colour not in use loosely across back of work. To avoid long, loose strands at back of work twist yarns every 4 or 5 sts *or* in foll row work under and over loose strands by inserting hook above and below strands after every 4 or 5 sts (see page 116).

▶ BACK
Panel 1

Using Tunisian hook and A, make 26ch. Beg Tunisian knit st as foll:
Base row Insert hook into 2nd ch from hook, yrh and draw a loop through, *insert hook into next ch, yrh and draw a loop through, rep from * to end of ch. Do not turn at end of rows. 26 loops on hook.
1st row (return row) Yrh and draw through first loop on hook, *yrh and draw through next 2 loops on hook, rep from * until there is one loop on hook (this forms first loop of next row).
2nd row (loop row) Miss first vertical loop in row below and insert hook from front to back through 2nd vertical loop (under the chain), yrh and draw a loop through, *insert hook through next vertical loop, yrh and draw a loop through, rep from * to end.
Note: To form a firm edge, insert hook through centre of last loop at edge making sure that there are 2 vertical strands of yarn on hook at extreme left-hand edge.
Last 2 rows form Tunisian knit st and are rep throughout. Cont in Tunisian

knit st until 3 loop rows more are completed, ending with a return row. Work first row of chart as foll:
Next row Using A, work as for loop row until there are 9 loops on hook, using B draw up next 7 loops, using A draw up next 10 loops. (See Note above.)
Next row Using A, yrh and draw through first loop on hook, (yrh and draw through next 2 loops on hook) 9

times, using B (yrh and draw through next 2 loops on hook) 7 times, using A (yrh and draw through next 2 loops on hook) 9 times.

Cont in this way, foll chart for loop rows (reading chart rows from right to left) and always drawing through a loop in a matching colour on return row, until 18 chart rows are completed, ending with a return row.

** Using A only, work 5 loop rows in patt, ending with a return row.

Work 18 chart rows, ending with a return row.**

Rep from ** to ** twice more. 4 motifs complete.

Using A only, work in patt until panel measures 54[55:56]cm from beg, ending with a return row.

Shoulder shaping

Next row Work as for loop row until there are 21 loops on hook, leaving rem sts unworked.

Work a return row on these sts. Dec 5 sts at end of next 3 loop rows in the same way, ending with a return row. 6 sts rem. Fasten off.

Panel 2

Using Tunisian hook and C, make 24[26:28]ch. Work base-2nd rows as for panel 1. 24[26:28] sts. Cont in Tunisian knit st until 3 loop rows more are completed, ending with a return row. Work next 18 rows foll chart and using C and D.

Using C only work 5 loop rows in patt, ending with a return row. Work 18 chart rows, ending with a return row.

Rep from *** to *** twice more. 4 motifs complete.

Using C only, work in patt until panel 2 has same number of loop rows as panel 1 to beg of shoulder shaping, ending with a return row.

Neck shaping

Using C, work first side of neck as foll:
****Next row** Work as for loop row until there are 4 loops on hook, leaving rem sts unworked.

Work a return row on these sts.

Next row Work as for loop row until 2 loops are on hook, miss next st and draw up a loop in last st.

Work a return row. Work one loop and one return row without shaping. Dec one st at end of next loop row. 2 loops on hook. Yrh and draw through 2 loops on hook. Fasten off.

Using C and with RS facing, draw up a loop in last 4 sts of row and work a return row.

Next row Miss first 2 vertical loops in row below and work as for loop row across last 2 sts. 3 loops on hook. Work a return row. Work one loop and one return row without shaping. Dec one st in the same way at beg of next loop row. 2 loops on hook. Yrh and draw a loop through 2 loops on hook. Fasten off.****

Panel 3

Work as for panel 1, reversing shoulder shaping by working decs at beg of row instead of end of row.

Panel 4

Using Tunisian hook and A, make 11[13:15]ch. Work base-2nd rows as for panel 1. 11[13:15] sts. Cont in Tunisian knit st, using A only, until panel measures 32cm from beg, ending with a return row.

Armhole shaping

Work as for panel 2 from **** to ****.

Panel 5

Work as for panel 4.

▶ **RIGHT FRONT**

Panel 6

Work as for panel 1 of back until first motif is complete, ending with a return row. Using A only, work one more loop and return row. Using ordinary crochet hook and A, work 1ch, 1dc into each vertical loop. Fasten off. This forms pocket.

Using Tunisian hook and A, make 26ch and work as for panel 1, omitting first motif, until panel 6 measures same as panel 1 to 2nd motif. Complete as for panel 1.

Panel 7

Work as for panel 2 of back until 3 motifs have been completed, then cont without shaping, using C only, until panel measures 40[41:42]cm from beg, ending with a return row. Break off C and fasten off.

Neck shaping

Next row Miss first 17[19:21] vertical loops in last row and using C, draw up a loop in each of last 7 sts.

Cont in Tunisian knit st until 2 more loop rows have been completed, ending with a return row.

Next row Miss first 2 vertical loops in row below and work as for loop row across last 5 sts. 6 loops on hook. Work 3 loop rows without shaping, ending with a return row. Dec one st at neck edge on next loop row and then on every 4th loop row 4 times in all. 2 sts. Work 2 loop rows more on these 2 sts, drawing through 2 loops on hook at end of 2nd loop row. Fasten off.

▶ **LEFT FRONT**

Panel 8

Using C, make 24[26:28]ch and work base-2nd rows as for panel 2. 24[26:28] sts.

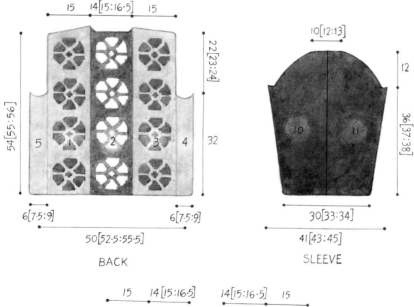

15   14[15:16·5]   15
22[23:24]
54[55:56]
5   1   2   3   4   32
6[7·5:9]   6[7·5:9]
50[52·5:55·5]
BACK

10[12:13]
12
36[37:38]
10   11
30[33:34]
41[43:45]
SLEEVE

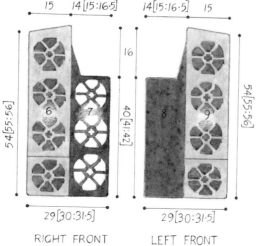

15   14[15:16·5]
16
54[55:56]
6   7
40[41:42]
29[30:31·5]
RIGHT FRONT

14[15:16·5]   15
54[55:56]
8   9
29[30:31·5]
LEFT FRONT

All measurements are in centimetres.

Work in Tunisian knit st, omitting motifs, until panel 8 measures same as panel 7 to neck shaping, ending with a return row.

Neck shaping

Next row Work as for loop row until there are 7 loops on hook.

Work a return row and complete neck shaping as for right front, reversing shaping.

Panel 9

Work as for panel 6, reversing shoulder shaping by working decs at beg of rows instead of end of row.

▶ **SLEEVES** (make 2)

Panel 10

Using C, make 26[28:29]ch. Work base- 2nd rows as for panel 1. Cont in Tunisian knit st, inc one st at end of every 7th loop row 9 times in all. 35[37:38] sts.

Note: Work inc by inserting hook under ch between last 2 sts of row and drawing a loop through to make an extra st, then working last (edge) st in usual way.

Work without shaping until panel measures 36[37:38]cm from beg, ending with a return row.

Sleeve top shaping

Next row Work as for loop row until there are 32[34:35] loops on hook, leaving rem sts unworked.

Work a return row. Dec one st at end of every alternate loop row 4 times, then one st at end of every loop row 10 times, then 2 sts at end of every loop row 5 times, ending with a return row. 8[10:11] sts.

Work one more loop and return row. Fasten off.

Panel 11

Work as for panel 10, reversing shaping by working incs and decs at beg of loop rows instead of at end.

▶ **COLLAR**

Using crochet hook and C, make 133ch.

Base row 1dc into 3rd ch from hook, *1ch, miss 1ch, 1dc into next ch, rep from * to end. Turn. 132 sts, counting each dc, each 1ch sp and turning ch as one st.

1st row 2ch, miss first dc, *1dc into next ch sp, 1ch, rep from *, ending with 1dc into 2ch sp at end. Turn.

Rep last row to form seed patt.

Cont in seed patt until collar measures 4.5cm from beg. Work one row in dc, working into each dc and each ch sp, then work one row in ss, inserting hook under both loops at top of dc. Fasten off.

Edging

Using D, make 133ch. Work base and first rows as for collar. Cont in seed patt until edging measures 2.5cm. Finish as for collar.

▶ **CUFFS** (make 2)

Using C, make 67[71:73]ch. Work base and first rows as for collar. 66[70:72] sts. Cont in seed patt until cuff measures 4.5cm from beg. Finish as for collar.

Edging

Using D, make 67[71:73]ch. Work as for cuff until edging measures 2.5cm. Finish as for collar.

▶ **MAKING UP**

Pin all Tunisian crochet pieces to correct measurements face down on a padded surface. Press on WS with a warm iron and damp cloth.

Pin pockets in place on panels 6 and 9. Sew panels tog foll diagram. Work seam by overlapping last st of one panel over first st of adjacent panel and working a running st through both layers in a matching colour. When joining panels 6 and 9, work through pockets and linings.

Join shoulder, sleeve and side seams. Set in sleeves.

Edging

Using crochet hook and C, work a row of dc evenly along horizontal straight edge at base of neck shaping on left front, down left front, then along lower edge changing to A when necessary to match colours, up right front and across base of neck, working 3dc at 4 corners and working through both thicknesses at base of pockets. Turn and work a 2nd row of dc into first. Fasten off.

Sew edgings to collar and cuffs, overlapping so that edging protrudes 2cm. Sew cuff seam. Sew on collar. Sew on cuffs, gathering lower sleeve to fit. Sew on hooks and eyes to fasten front. Sew in shoulder pads if desired. Press seams lightly on WS.

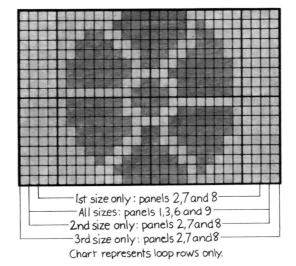

1st size only: panels 2, 7 and 8
All sizes: panels 1, 3, 6 and 9
2nd size only: panels 2, 7 and 8
3rd size only: panels 2, 7 and 8

Chart represents loop rows only.

BOBBLED FAIR ISLE

Treble crochet bobbles and Tunisian stitch fans give this pretty jacket the look of Fair Isle knitting. The contrast of shiny mercerised cotton and soft wool adds texture to the crochet fabric.

Note: When working dc in colour patt, always insert hook through both loops of the top of the dc of the last row in the usual way except where specifically stated otherwise. When changing

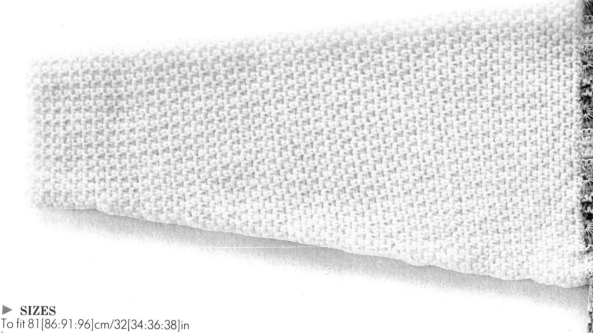

▶ SIZES

To fit 81[86:91:96]cm/32[34:36:38]in bust.
Note: Figures for larger sizes are in square brackets. If there is only one set of figures, it applies to all sizes.
See diagram for finished measurements.

▶ MATERIALS

See page 118 for further yarn information
Use a lightweight wool yarn (approx 200m per 50g) and a lightweight cotton yarn (approx 185m per 50g):
200[250:250]g lightweight wool yarn in A (white)
100[150:150]g lightweight wool yarn in B (dusty pink)
50g lightweight wool yarn in each of C (grey green) and D (pale grey)
100g lightweight cotton yarn in E (pale aqua)
50g lightweight cotton yarn in each of F (pale lilac), G (cherry) and H (pink)
4.00mm, 4.50mm and 5.00mm crochet hooks *or sizes to obtain correct tensions*
Shoulder pads (optional)

▶ TENSION

21 sts to 10cm and 32 row patt rep to 19cm over colour patt using 4.50mm hook for fan rows and 4.00mm hook for all other patt rows.
21 sts and 22 rows to 10cm over seed patt using 5.00mm hook (for sleeves).
Check your tensions before beginning (see Note above).

colours in a row, change to new colour with last yrh of previous dc thus closing last st with new colour (see page 112). To check tension over colour patt make 28ch, using A and 4.00mm hook. Work one row in dc. 27dc. Then work 1st-34th rows of colour patt. To check tension over seed patt make 27ch, using A and 5.00mm hook. Work base-1st rows of seed patt as for beg of back. Then cont in seed patt until piece measures 12cm.

▶ BACK

Using 4.50mm hook and A, make 111[117:123:129]ch. Beg seed patt as foll:
Base row 1dc into 3rd ch from hook, *1ch, miss 1ch, 1dc into next ch, rep from * to end. Turn. 110[116:122:128] sts, counting each dc, each ch sp and turning ch as one st.
1st row 2ch, 1dc into first ch sp, 1ch, 1dc into next ch sp, rep from *, ending with 1ch, 1dc into 2ch sp at end. Turn. Last row forms seed patt.
2nd-5th rows Rep first row 4 times more.
6th row Using 4.00mm hook, 1ch, 2dc into first dc, *1dc into next ch sp, 1dc into next dc, rep from *, ending with 1dc into 2ch sp at end. Turn. 111[117:123:129]dc.
This completes seed patt edging.
Beg colour patt as foll:
1st patt row (fan row) (RS) Using 4.50mm hook and B, 1ch, miss first dc,

(insert hook into next dc, yrh and draw a loop through) 3 times — 4 loops on hook, yrh and draw through 1 loop on hook, (yrh and draw through 2 loops on hook) 3 times — 4 Tunisian sts made, draw E through loop and drop and tighten B, 4ch, miss first ch and draw up a loop *loosely* into each of rem E chs, draw up a loop *loosely* into each of first 3 Tunisian sts inserting hook from right to left through vertical bar of each st and leaving last Tunisian st unworked — 7 loops on hook, yrh and draw through all 7 loops (fan), 1ch for eye, *draw B through loop and

drop and tighten E, draw up a loop into eye of fan just made, 1 loop into back of last loop of fan, 1 loop into vertical bar of last unworked Tunisian st, 1 loop in each of next 3dc — 7 loops on hook, yrh and draw through 1 loop on hook, (yrh and draw through 2 loops on hook) 6 times — 7 Tunisian sts made, draw E through loop and drop B, draw up a loop into each of first 6 vertical bars of Tunisian sts, yrh and draw through all 7 loops on hook, 1ch for eye, rep from *, ending draw B through loop and drop E, draw up a loop into eye of fan just made, 1 loop

into back of last loop of fan, 1 loop into vertical bar of last unworked Tunisian st, 1 loop into each of last 2dc — 6 loops on hook, yrh and draw through 1 loop on hook, (yrh and draw through 2 loops on hook) 5 times — 6 Tunisian sts made, draw E through loop and drop B, draw up a loop into each of last 6 vertical bars of Tunisian sts, yrh and draw through all 7 loops on hook, 1ch, draw B through loop and drop E. Turn.

2nd row Using 4.00mm hook and B, 1ch, 1dc into eye of first fan, *1dc into top loop of same fan, 1dc into top of next Tunisian st, 1dc into eye of next fan, rep from *, ending with 1dc into top loop of last fan, 1dc into top of E ch. Turn. 111[117:123:129]dc.

Note: Always count sts at end of last row to make sure that there are correct number of sts.

Cont with 4.00mm hook until next fan row is reached.

3rd and 4th rows Using F, 1ch, 1dc into each dc to end. Turn.

5th row Using A, 1ch, working into *back* loops only, 1dc into each dc to end. Turn.

6th row Using A, 1ch, 1dc into first dc, *1dc into next dc but inserting hook through *front* loop only, 1dc into each of next 3dc, rep from *, ending with 1dc into each rem dc to end. Turn.

7th row (bobble row) Using A, 1ch, 1dc into each dc to first of missed loops of last row, changing to G with last yrh of last dc, *miss dc above missed loop, (yrh, insert hook from bottom to top through missed loop, yrh and draw a loop through, yrh and draw through 2 loops on hook) 5 times — 6 loops on hook, drop G and using A draw through all 6 loops on hook — called bobble —, carrying G across top of last row and working all sts over it, work 1dc into each of next 3dc, rep from *, ending last rep with 1dc into last dc. Turn.

8th row Using A, 1ch, 1dc into each dc and each bobble. Turn.

9th and 10th rows As 3rd and 4th rows.

11th row As first row of colour patt, but inserting hook through *back* loops only when working into dc of last row.

12th row As 2nd row.

13th row Using C, 1ch, 1dc into each of next 2dc changing to A with last yrh of last dc, using A, 1dc into each of next 2dc changing to C with last yrh of last dc, cont in this way working 2dc in C and 2dc in A alternately until row is complete. Turn.

14th-16th rows 1ch, work all dc in A in C and all dc in C in A, thus reversing positions of C and A in each row. Turn.

17th and 18th rows As first and 2nd rows of colour patt.

19th and 20th rows Using H, work in dc. Turn.

21st row Using D, work in dc working

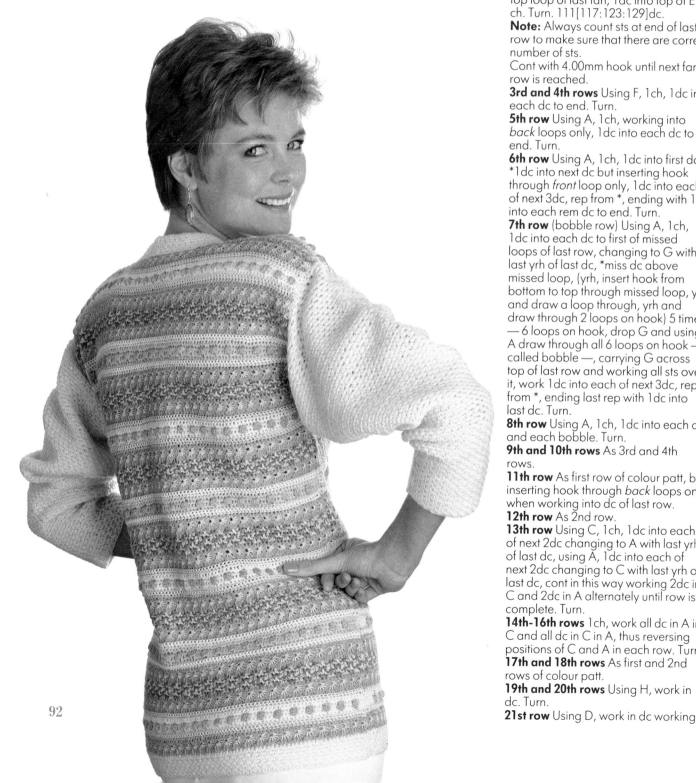

into *back* loops only. Turn.
22nd and 23rd rows As 6th and 7th rows.
24th row Using D, as 8th row.
25th-26th rows As 19th and 20th rows.
27th-34th rows As 11th-18th rows.
Rep 3rd-34th colour patt rows to form colour patt.
Cont in colour patt until back measures 69[70:71:72]cm from beg. Fasten off.

▶ **FRONTS** (make 2)
Using 4.50mm hook and A, make 43[45:49:51]ch and work base and first rows as for seed patt on back. 42[44:48:50] sts. Work 2nd-6th rows as for seed patt on back inc one st on 6th row for *2nd and 4th sizes only.* 42[45:48:51]dc.
Beg with first colour patt row of back, complete as for back.

▶ **SLEEVES** (make 2)
Using 5.00mm hook and A, make 57ch and work base and first rows as for seed patt on back. 56 sts.
**Work 6[5:5:5] rows more in seed patt.
Next row (inc row) 2ch, 1dc into first dc, 1ch, 1dc into first ch sp, work in patt across row, ending with (1dc, 1ch, 1dc) all into 2ch sp. Turn. 4 sts increased.** 60 sts.
Rep from ** to ** 11[12:13:13] times more. 104[108:112:112] sts. Work in seed patt without shaping until sleeve measures 45cm from beg or desired sleeve length. Fasten off.

▶ **FRONT BANDS** (make 2)
Using 5.00mm hook and A, make 161[163:165:167]ch and work base and first rows as for seed patt on back. 160[162:164:166] sts. Work 4 rows more in seed patt. Fasten off.

▶ **MAKING UP**
Do not press. Darn in all loose ends. Join shoulder seams leaving 16cm free at centre back for back neck. Sew on front bands from lower edge of fronts to centre back neck. Sew seam of band at centre back. Mark positions of sleeves 25[26:27:27]cm from shoulder seams. Sew on sleeves between markers. Join side and sleeve seams. Press seams lightly on WS with warm iron. If desired, sew in shoulder pads.

DESIGN VARIATIONS

▶ **WAISTCOAT**
For a waistcoat work back and fronts as for cardigan. For armbands make 117ch and work as for front band. Make up as for cardigan, omitting sleeves and leaving 28cm open from shoulder seams for armbands. Join armband seam and sew in place.

▶ **PULLOVER**
For a pullover work back and front alike. Make up as for cardigan omitting front bands and leaving 28cm open for neck. Then make neckband as for a single armband. Join neckband seam and sew in place.

53[56:58:61]

BACK

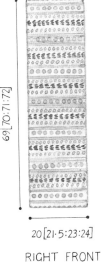

69[70:71:72]

20[21·5:23:24]

RIGHT FRONT

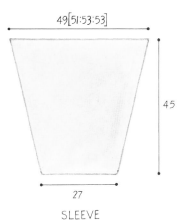

49[51:53:53]

45

27

SLEEVE

All measurements are in centimetres.

WAVES & CHECKS

The patterns on this sweater, crocheted in a slubbed cotton yarn, are made by varying the stitch heights and by using overlapping, elongated double crochet which means only one colour is used in each row. A slipover variation can be made from this pattern by omitting the sleeves.

▶ **SIZES**
To fit 81[86:91:96]cm/32[34:36:38]in bust.
Note: Figures for larger sizes are in square brackets. If there is only one set of figures, it applies to all sizes. *See diagram for finished measurements.*

▶ **MATERIALS**
See page 118 for further yarn information
Use a medium weight slubbed cotton yarn (100m per 50g):
350[350:400:450]g in A (lilac)
150[150:200:200]g in each of B (light blue) and D (pink)
200[250:250:250]g in C (purple)
100g in E (coral)
5.00mm crochet hook *or size to obtain correct tension*

► TENSION

16 sts to 10cm over patt and 18 rows of patt rep to 9cm using 5.00mm hook. 18dc and 20 rows to 10cm over rib patt using 5.00mm hook.
Check your tensions before beginning.

Note: To check tension make 20ch and work base-18th rows of back foll instructions for first size. Make sure that the elongated dc sts are worked *loosely* so that they do not pull the fabric tog.

► BACK

Using A, make 80[84:88:92]ch.
Base row Using A, 1dc into 2nd ch from hook, 1dc into each dc to end. Turn. 79[83:87:91]dc.
1st row Using A, 1ch, 1dc into each dc to end. Turn.

2nd row As first row.
3rd row Using B, 1ch, 1dc into each of first 3dc, working next 2 sts into rows below insert hook from front through top of dc 2 rows below next dc, yrh and draw a loop through pulling loop up to height of previous row so that fabric is not pulled tog, yrh and draw through 2 loops on hook — called 1dc into next dc 2 rows below —, *1dc into each of next 2dc, (1dc into next dc 2 rows below) twice, rep from *, ending with 1dc into each of last 2dc. Turn.

4th row Using B, as first row.
5th row Using A, as first row.
6th row Using A, 1ch, 1dc into first dc, 1dc into next dc 2 rows below, *1dc into each of next 2dc, (1dc into next dc 2 rows below) twice, rep from *, ending with 1dc into last dc. Turn. Using C, work 4 rows in dc.
11th row Using D, 1ch, 1dc into first dc, *1dc into next dc one row below, 1dc into next dc 2 rows below, 1dc into next dc 3 rows below, 1dc into next dc 2 rows below, 1dc into next dc one row below, 1dc into next dc, rep from * to last dc, 1dc into last dc. Turn. Using D, work 3 rows in dc.
15th row Using C, as for 11th row. Using C, work one row in dc.
17th row Using B, 1ch, 1dc into first st, *1htr into next st, 1tr into next st, 1dtr into next st, 1tr into next st, 1htr into next st, 1dc into next st, rep from *, ending with 0[1:1:0]htr into next st, 0[1:1:0]tr into next st, 0[1:0:0]dtr into next st, 0[1:0:0]tr into next st. Turn.
18th row Using E, 5[2:2:5]ch, miss first st, 0[1:0:0]dc into next st, 0[1:0:0]htr into next st, 0[1:1:0]tr into next st, 0[1:1:0]dtr into next st, *1tr into next st, 1htr into next st, 1dc into next st, 1htr into next st, 1tr into next st, 1dtr into next st, rep from * to end, working last st into turning ch. Turn.
19th row Using A, as first row working last dc into turning ch. 2nd-19th rows form patt and are repeated throughout. Cont in patt until back measures 53[54:55:56]cm from beg. Fasten off.

► FRONT

Work as for back until front measures 24[25:26:27]cm from beg.
Neck shaping
Keeping to patt as set, beg neck shaping as foll:

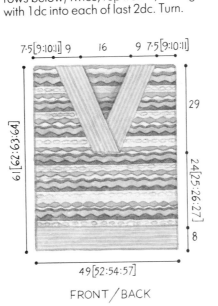

7·5[9:10:11] 9 16 9 7·5[9:10:11]

29

61[62:63:64]

24[25:26:27]

8

49[52:54:57]

FRONT/BACK

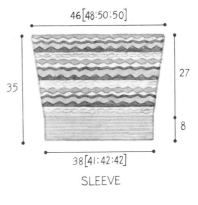

46[48:50:50]

35

27

8

38[41:42:42]

SLEEVE

All measurements are in centimetres.

Next row Work in patt across first 32[34:36:38]sts. Turn, leaving rem sts unworked.
Cont on these sts, dec one st at neck edge on every 2nd and 3rd rows alternately 10 times in all.
22[24:26:28] sts. Dec one st at neck edge every 3rd row 10 times.
12[14:16:18] sts. Cont without shaping until front measures same as back to shoulder. Fasten off.

Miss centre 15 sts and work in patt across last 32[34:36:38] sts.
Work 2nd side of neck as for first side, reversing shaping.

▶ **SLEEVES** (make 2)
Using A, make 62[66:68:68]ch and work base-2nd rows as for back. 61[65:67:67]dc.
3rd row Using B, 1ch, 1dc into each of first 3dc, *(1dc into next dc 2 rows

A sleeveless variation makes a loose summer vest in crisp contrasting tones of black, white and grey.

below) twice, 1dc into each of next 2dc, rep from *, ending with 1[1:0:0]dc into dc 2 rows below next dc, 1[1:0:0]dc into next dc. Turn.
Cont working in patt as for back *and at the same time* inc one st at each end of 7th row and then every 8th[8th:7th:7th] row 6[6:7:7] times in all. 73[77:81:81] sts.
Cont in patt without shaping until sleeve measures 27cm from beg. Fasten off.

▶ **BACK RIB**
Using A, make 87[92:96:101]ch.
Base row 1dc into 2nd ch from hook, 1dc into each ch to end. Turn. 86[91:95:100]dc.
1st row 1ch, working into *back* loops only throughout, 1dc into each dc to end. Turn.
Rep last row to form rib patt. Work 14 rows more in rib patt. Fasten off.

▶ **FRONT RIB**
Work as for back rib.

▶ **NECKBANDS**
Using A, make 56ch and work base and first rows as for back rib. 55dc.
*2nd row** 1ch, 2dc into first dc, 1dc into each dc to last 2dc, (insert hook into next dc, yrh and draw a loop through) twice — called 2dc tog. Turn.
Rep first row 3 times.*
Rep from * to * twice more, rep 2nd row once, rep first row once.
Fasten off.

▶ **SLEEVE BANDS** (make 2)
Using A, make 67[73:76:76]ch and work base and first rows as for back rib. 66[72:75:75]dc. Work 14 rows more in rib as for back rib. Fasten off.

▶ **MAKING UP**
Do not press. Darn in all loose ends. Join shoulder seams. Sew ribs to back and front. Sew sleeve bands to sleeves. Mark positions for sleeves 23[24:25:25]cm from shoulder seams. Sew on sleeves between markers. Join side and sleeve seams. Sew neckbands in place overlapping right neckband over left neckband at centre front. Press lightly on WS, avoiding ribs.

DESIGN VARIATION

▶ **SLEEVELESS TOP**
For a sleeveless top follow instructions omitting sleeves and sleevebands. For armhole bands make 92ch and work base and 1st rows as for back rib. Work in rib patt for 6 rows more and fasten off. Sew armhole band seams. Make up as for version with sleeves, omitting sleeves and leaving 26cm from shoulder seams open for armholes. Sew on armhole bands.

OPENWORK

OPENWORK

Crochet lace is probably the most well-known crochet fabric and it is still popular as bedspreads, tablecloths and edgings for sheets and pillowcases. Using lace collars and cuffs on garments goes in and out of fashion but there are other equally effective ways of using crochet openwork for sweaters. The advantage of working open crochet stitches rather than solid stitches is that the resulting fabric is lighter and provides an attractive drape. It is best to stick to the stitches that are not too transparent unless you really want a see-through effect.

▶ **ADDING COLOUR**

Most crocheters are conditioned to think of lacy fabrics in white or ecru cotton yarn, unaware of how stunning a splash of colour can be. There is no need to restrict openwork to smooth cotton. Fuzzier yarns such as chenille or mohair are particularly striking for widely spaced stitches because the fibres extend into the open holes. Variations on the bobbled zigzag patterns on *Bobbled lace* (page 103) are given here (3 and 5). They translate easily onto the simple top because the top is merely two rectangles and requires no neck or armhole shaping. The pattern with vertical stripes (4) is

for more advanced crocheters. Each vertical stripe is worked with a separate length of yarn. A simpler way to introduce colour is with horizontal stripes so that each colour is worked over two rows (5).

▶ **MOTIFS ON FILET**

Filet crochet should not be seen as merely curtain fabric. Colour patterns or motifs can transform a simple filet net into a perfect fashion fabric. Again stripes are the simplest colour design. The net ground is also an ideal base for weaving (see page 113) or for applied motifs. The motifs here (1), worked onto a striped filet net, are little rectangles in surface slip stitch (see page 111). Motifs can be charted and worked into the basic net fabric (2). Both of these designs are alternatives for the chequered pattern on *Chenille chequers* (page 106).

▶ **BOBBLES ON FILET**

Contrasting bobble patterns on filet (4) are designed by charting bobble shapes or outlines onto a graph paper so that each square represents a chain space. The bobbles are worked into the centre of the space. The sample shown here is another possible design variation for *Chenille chequers* (page 106).

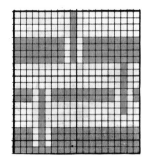

1 Worked in htr filet net (see symbol chart) with added ss motifs following chart above for stripe sequence and placement of ss motifs. Each square represents a ch space.

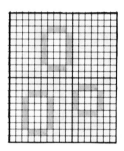

2 Worked in htr filet net (see symbol chart) following chart above for colours. Each square represents a ch space.

1   2

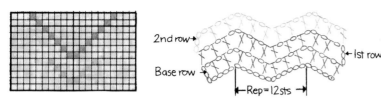

Foundation ch = multiple of 12ch plus one.

5 Repeat 2nd row to form patt, working 2 rows in each colour alternately. Weave 4 strands of a contrasting yarn up centre of every other zigzag.

3 Worked in htr filet net (see symbol chart) with bobbles following chart above for placement of bobbles. Each square represents a ch space or a bobble. (See page 111 for bobbles.)

Symbol chart for filet net (1, 2 and 3)

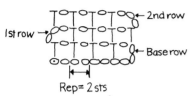

Foundation ch = odd number of ch.
Rep 2nd row to form patt.

4 See page 103 for symbol chart to work openwork zigzag patt with bobbles. Use a separate ball of yarn for each zigzag to form vertical stripes and use a short length of contrasting colour for each bobble.

5

3

4

SCALLOPED LACE

This soft mohair sweater is very quick to make. It is worked in a combination of trebles, double crochet and chain stitches which form a simple openwork pattern. The sweater can be worn with or without the cowl neck, which is made separately.

▶ **SIZES**

To fit 81[86-91:96-102]cm/32[34-36: 38-40]in bust.

Note: Figures for larger sizes are in square brackets. If there is only one set of figures, it applies to all sizes. *See diagram for finished measurements.*

▶ **MATERIALS**

See page 118 for further yarn information

Use a lightweight silk and mohair yarn (approx 60m per 20g):
220[240:280]g in main colour MC (white)
60[60:80]g in each of 3 contrasting colours A (yellow), B (pink) and C (pale lilac)
4.00mm and 4.50mm crochet hooks *or sizes to obtain correct tensions*

▶ TENSION

6 V sts (or six 4ch spaces) and 11 rows to 10cm over lace patt using 4.00mm hook.

18dc and 18 rows to 10cm over rib patt using 4.50mm hook.

Check your tensions before beginning (see Note below).

▶ BACK AND FRONT (alike)

Using smaller hook and MC, make 104[107:110]ch and beg at side seam as foll:

Base row 1dc into 2nd ch from hook, *4ch, miss 2ch, 1dc into next ch, rep from * to end. Turn. 34[35:36] 4ch spaces.

1st row Using A, 5ch, 1tr into first 4ch sp, *(1tr, 1ch, 1tr — called V st) all into next 4ch sp, rep from * to end. Turn. 34[35:36] V sts, counting 5ch and first tr as first V st.

2nd row Using A, 1ch, 1dc into first tr, 4ch, 1dc into sp between first 2 V sts, *4ch, 1dc into sp between next 2 V sts, rep from *, ending last rep with 1dc into 5ch sp. Turn.

Last 2 rows form lace patt. Cont in lace patt, working next 2 rows in B, then 2 rows in C and 3[5:7] rows in MC.

Neck shaping

Using MC, beg to shape neck as foll:

Next row Work ss loosely across top of first 2 V sts, 1dc into sp between 2nd and 3rd V sts, work in patt to end. Turn. Two 4ch sps decreased. 32[33:34] 4ch sps.

Next row Work in patt to last 4ch sp. Turn. One V st decreased.

All measurements are in centimetres.

31[32:33]V sts.

Rep last 2 rows once more. 28[29:30] V sts.

Next row Work ss loosely across top of first V st, 1dc into sp between first and 2nd V sts, work in patt to end. Turn. 27[28:29] 4ch sps.

Next row Using A, work in patt without dec. Turn.

Rep last 2 rows 3 times more, working in stripes of one row A, 2 rows B, 2 rows C and one row MC. 24[25:26] V sts.

Using MC, work 11 rows in patt without shaping. Work one row A.

Next row Using A, 4ch, 1dc into 2nd ch from hook, 4ch, miss 2ch, 1dc into first tr, work in patt to end. Turn. One 4ch sp increased. 25[26:27] 4ch sps.

Next row Using B, work in patt without inc. Turn.

Rep last 2 rows twice more, working one row B, 2 rows C and one row MC. 27[28:29] V sts.

Using MC, cont to shape neck as foll:

Next row Inc one 4ch sp at beg of row, work in patt to end. Turn.

Next row Work in patt to end of row, then work one more V st into last 4ch sp. Turn. 29[30:31] V sts.

Next row 7ch, 1dc into 2nd ch from hook, 4ch, miss 2ch, 1dc into next ch, 4ch, 1dc into first tr, work in patt to end. Turn. 31[32:33] 4ch sps.

Rep last 2 rows once more. 34[35:36] 4ch sps.

Cont in patt without shaping, working 2[4:6] rows MC, then 2 rows A, 2 rows B, 2 rows C and one row MC. Fasten off.

▶ SLEEVES (make 2)

Using smaller hook and C, make 14[17:17]ch and work base row as for back. 4[5:5] 4ch sps.

1st row Using B, 5ch, 1tr into first 4ch sp, *1 V st into next 4ch sp, rep from * to end, then work 1 more V st into last 4ch sp. Turn. 5[6:6] V sts.

2nd row Using B, 13ch, 1dc into 2nd ch from hook, (4ch, miss 2ch, 1dc into next ch) 3 times, 4ch, 1dc into first tr, work in patt to end. Turn. 9[10:10] 4ch sps.

Rep last 2 rows 3 times more, working 2 rows A and 4 rows MC. 24[25:25] 4ch sps.

Cont in patt without shaping, working

Note: Back, front and sleeves are worked in rows which progress from side seam to side seam instead of from lower edge to top in the usual way. To check tension make 26ch using MC and work base-2nd rows of back or foll symbol chart. Cont in patt until work measures 12cm.

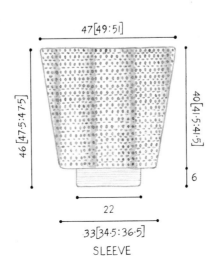

9[11:12.5] 31 9[11:12.5]

16.5

63.5[65.5:67]

40[42:43.5]

7

45[48:51]

49[53:56]

FRONT/BACK

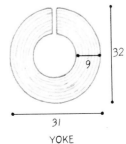

47[49:51]

46[47.5:47.5]

40[41.5:41.5]

6

22

33[34.5:36.5]

SLEEVE

32

9

31

YOKE

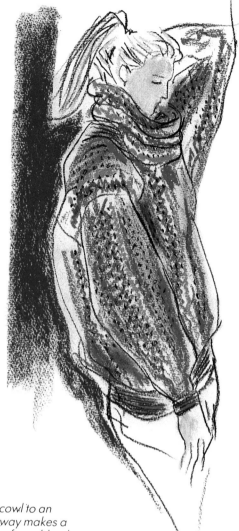

The addition of a cowl to an alternative colourway makes a softly snug sweater for colder days.

6 rows more MC, 2 rows C, 2 rows B, 2 rows A, 10[12:14] rows MC, 2 rows C, 2 rows B, 2 rows A and 7 rows MC, so ending with a V st row.
Using MC, beg shaping 2nd side of sleeve as foll:
Next row Work ss loosely across top of first 4 V sts, 1dc into sp between 4th and 5th V sts, work in patt to end. Turn. 20[21:21] 4ch sps.
Next row Work in patt to last 4ch sp. Turn. 19[20:20] V sts.
Rep last 2 rows 3 times more, working one row more MC, 2 rows C, 2 rows B, one row A. Fasten off.

▶ BACK RIB
Using larger hook and MC, make 82[87:93]ch.
Base row 1dc into 2nd ch from hook, 1dc into each ch to end. Turn. 81[86:92]dc.
1st row (WS) 1ch, working into *front* loop only of each dc, 1dc into each dc to end. Turn.
2nd row (RS) 1ch, working into *back* loop only of each dc, 1dc into each dc to end. Turn.
Last 2 rows form rib patt. Work in rib patt until rib measures 7cm from beg. Fasten off.

▶ FRONT RIB
Work as for back rib.

▶ CUFFS (make 2)
Using larger hook and MC, make 40ch. Work base-2nd rows as for back rib. 39dc. Cont in rib patt until cuff measures 6cm from beg. Fasten off.

▶ YOKE
Using larger hook and MC, make 179ch and work base and first rows as for back rib. 178dc.
2nd row (RS) 1ch, working into *back* loop only of each dc, 1dc into each of first 10dc, (insert hook into next dc, yrh and draw a loop through) twice, yrh and draw through all 3 loops on hook

— called 2dc tog —, *1dc into each of next 10dc, 2dc tog*, rep from * to * 12 times more, 1dc into each dc to end. Turn. 164dc.
3rd row As first row.
4th row 1ch, working into *back* loop only of each dc, 1dc into each dc dec 14 sts evenly across row. Turn. 150dc.
Rep last 2 rows 5 times more. 80dc.
Next row As first row.
Fasten off.

▶ COWL
Using smaller hook and MC, make 95ch. Work base row as for back rib. 94dc.
**1st row Using A, 5ch, 1tr into first dc, *miss 2dc, (1tr, 1ch, 1tr) all into next dc, rep from * to end. Turn. 32 V sts.
2nd row Using A, as for 2nd row of back. Turn.
3rd row Using B, 5ch, 1tr into first 4ch sp, *(1tr, 2ch, 1tr — called V st) all into next 4ch sp, rep from * to end. Turn.
4th row Using B, 1ch, 1dc into first tr, 5ch, 1dc into sp between first 2 V sts, *5ch, 1dc into sp between next 2 V sts, rep from *, ending last rep with 1dc into 5ch sp. Turn.
Rep last 2 rows 3 times more, working V sts into 5ch sps and working 2 rows more in B, then 4 rows in C.
Next row Using MC, 3ch, 1dc into first 5ch sp, *3dc into next 5ch sp, rep from * to end. 94dc.
Using MC, work one row in dc.**
Rep from ** to ** 2 times more.
Next row Using MC, 3ch, miss first 2dc, 1tr into each of next 2dc, *miss next dc, 1tr into each of next 2dc, rep from * to end.
Work one row in dc. Fasten off.

▶ MAKING UP
Do not press. Join shoulder seams. Mark positions of sleeves 23[24:25]cm from shoulder seams. Sew on sleeves between markers. Sew on cuffs and back and front ribs, easing in fullness. Join side and sleeve seams. Sew centre back yoke seam. Sew yoke to neck edge with seam at centre back. Using smaller hook and A and with RS facing, work one row of dc evenly around neck edge. Join with a ss to first dc. Fasten off.
Join cowl seam.

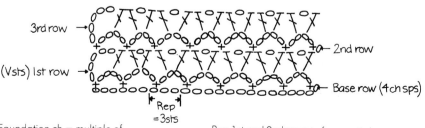

Foundation ch = multiple of 3ch plus 2 extra.

Rep 1st and 2nd rows to form patt.

BOBBLED LACE

Treble bobbles dot the openwork zigzags of this loose-fitting off-the-shoulder top. The simple lace pattern is worn over a body-hugging crochet rib top with a high neckline which snaps together.

▶ SIZES
To fit 81-86[91:96-102]cm/32-34[36: 38-40]in bust.
Note: Figures for larger sizes are in square brackets. If there is only one set of figures, it applies to all sizes.
See diagram for finished measurements.

▶ MATERIALS
See page 118 for further yarn information
Use a lightweight cotton yarn (approx 185m per 50g):
390[440:490]g for lace top
280[320:380]g for ribbed top
3.50mm crochet hook *or size to obtain correct tensions*
Snap fasteners

▶ TENSION
20tr to 9cm over lace patt using 3.50mm hook.
23dc and 30 rows to 10cm over rib patt using 3.50mm hook.
Check your tensions before beginning.

Note: Back and front of ribbed top are worked in rows which progress from side seam to side seam instead of from lower edge to top in the usual way. To check tension make 36ch and work base-4th rows of back or foll symbol chart. Cont in patt until sample measures 12cm.

LACE TOP

▶ BACK AND FRONT (alike)
Make 132[144:156]ch.
Base row 1tr into 4th ch from hook, 1tr into each of next 3ch, 2ch, 1tr into each of next 5ch, *miss 2ch, 1tr into each of next 5ch, 2ch, 1tr into each of next 5ch, rep from * to end. Turn.
110[120:130]tr, counting turning ch as first tr.
1st row (RS) 4ch, miss first 3tr and work 1tr into 4th tr, 1ch, miss next tr, 1tr into first of next 2ch, 1ch; 5tr into same ch as last tr was worked, remove hook and insert through top of first tr of 5tr group, draw working loop through — called bobble —, *1ch, 1tr into next ch, (1ch, miss next tr, 1tr into next tr) twice, miss next 2tr, (1tr into next tr, 1ch, miss next tr) twice, 1tr into first of next 2ch, 1ch, 1 bobble into same ch as last tr, rep from *, ending with 1ch, 1tr into next ch, 1ch, miss next tr, 1tr into next tr, 1ch, miss last 2tr, 1tr into 3rd of 3ch.

Turn.
2nd row 3ch, miss first tr and first 1ch sp, (1tr into next tr, 1tr into next 1ch sp) twice, *2ch, miss st at top of bobble, (1tr into next 1ch sp, 1tr into next tr) twice, 1tr into next 1ch sp, miss next 2tr, (1tr into next 1ch sp, 1tr into next tr) twice, 1tr into next 1ch sp, rep from *, ending with 2ch, miss st at top of bobble, (1tr into next 1ch sp, 1tr into next tr) twice, 1tr into 3rd of 4ch. Turn.
3rd row 3ch, miss first 2tr, 1tr into each of next 3tr, *1tr into first of next 2ch, 1ch, 1 bobble into same ch as last tr, 1ch, 1tr into next ch, 1tr into each of next 4tr, miss 2tr, 1tr into each of next 4tr, rep from *, ending with 1tr into first of next 2ch, 1ch, 1 bobble into same ch as last tr, 1ch, 1tr into next ch, 1tr into each of next 3tr, miss last tr, 1tr into 3rd of 4ch. Turn.
4th row 3ch, miss first 2tr, 1tr into each of next 3tr, *1tr into next 1ch sp, 2ch, miss st at top of bobble, 1tr into next 1ch sp, 1tr into each of next 4tr, miss next 2tr, 1tr into each of next 4tr, rep from *, ending with 1tr into next 1ch sp, 2ch, miss st at top of bobble, 1tr into next 1ch sp, 1tr into each of next 3tr, miss last tr, 1tr into 3rd of 3ch. Turn.

First-4th rows form lace patt. Cont in lace patt until work measures 56[58:60]cm from beg, ending with a 2nd or a 4th row.
Work a finishing row as foll:
Last row (RS) 3ch, miss first tr, 1tr into next tr, 1htr into each of next 2tr, 1dc into next tr, 1dc into 2ch sp, *1dc into next tr, 1htr into each of next 2tr, 1tr into each of next 4tr, 1htr into each of next 2tr, 1dc into next tr, 1dc into 2ch sp, rep from *, ending with 1dc into next tr, 1htr into each of next 2tr, 1tr into last tr, 1tr into 3rd of 3ch. Fasten off.

▶ MAKING UP
Do not press. Join shoulder seams, leaving 32cm open at centre for neck opening. Join side seams, leaving 22[23:24]cm open at top for armholes. Work a row of dc evenly around armholes, join with a ss to first dc and fasten off.

RIBBED TOP

▶ BACK
Side shaping
** Make 10ch and beg shaped piece at underarm as foll:
Base row (RS) 1dc into 2nd ch from hook, 1dc into each ch to end. Turn.
9dc.

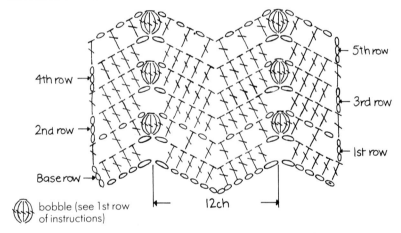

bobble (see 1st row of instructions)

Foundation ch = multiple of 12ch.

Rep 1st-4th rows to form patt.

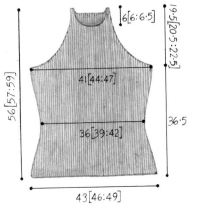

FRONT / BACK

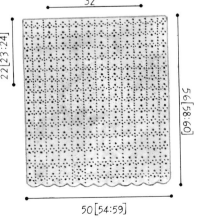

TUNIC FRONT / BACK

All measurements are in centimetres.

1st row (WS) 9ch, 1dc into 2nd ch from hook, 1dc into each of next 7ch, working into *back* loops only work 1dc into each dc to end. Turn. 17dc.
2nd row 1ch, working into *back* loops only, work 1dc into each dc to end. Turn.
Rib patt is formed by working dc into *back* loops only throughout. Cont in rib patt as foll:
3rd row As first row. 25dc.
4th row As 2nd row.
Rep last 2 rows once more, so ending with a RS row. 33dc. Break off yarn and set piece aside.
Make 17ch and work base row as for first piece. 16dc.
Next row (WS) As 2nd row.
Next row (RS) 5ch, 1dc into 2nd ch from hook, 1dc into each of next 3ch, work in rib patt to end. Turn. 20dc.
Rep last 2 rows 3 times more. 32dc.
Joining and armhole shaping
Join to first piece as foll:
Next row (WS) Work in rib patt to end, do not turn, make 19ch, then cont in rib patt across first piece. Turn.
Next row (RS) 1ch, 2dc into first dc (armhole edge), work in rib patt to end, working 1dc into each ch. Turn. 85dc.
Work one row without shaping.
Next row 1ch, 2dc into first dc, work in

rib patt to end. Turn. 86dc.
Work one row without shaping.
Rep last 2 rows 0[2:2] times more, so ending at armhole edge. 86[88:88]dc.
Inc one st at armhole edge on next and every foll row 20[20:24] times in all, so ending at armhole edge. 106[108:112]dc.
Next row 1ch, 2dc into each of first 2dc, work in rib patt to end. Turn. 108[110:114]dc.
Next row Work in patt to last 2dc, 2dc into each of last 2dc. Turn. 110[112:116]dc.
Rep last 2 rows 3 times more, so ending at armhole edge. 122[124:128]dc.
Next row 8[8:9]ch, 1dc into 2nd ch from hook, 1dc into each of next 6[6:7]ch, work in patt to end. Turn. 129[131:136]dc.
Work one row without shaping. Break off yarn.**
Neck shaping
Next row Miss first 3[3:4]dc and rejoin yarn to next dc with a ss, 1ch, 1dc into same place as ss, work in patt to end. Turn. 126[128:132]dc.
Next row Work in patt to last 2dc, (insert hook into next dc, yrh and draw a loop through) twice, yrh and draw through all 3 loops on hook — called

2dc tog. Turn. 125[127:131]dc.
Next row 1ch, 2dc tog, work in patt to end. Turn. 124[126:130]dc.
Work 35[35:37] rows without shaping, so ending at neck edge. Inc one st at neck edge on next 2 rows. 126[128:132]dc.
Next row 4[4:5]ch, 1dc into 2nd ch from hook, 1dc into each of next 2[2:3]ch, work in patt to end. Turn. 129[131:136]dc.
***Work one row without shaping. Break off yarn.
Armhole shaping
Next row Miss first 7[7:8]dc and rejoin yarn to next dc with a ss, 1ch, 1dc into same place as ss, work in patt to end. Turn. 122[124:128]dc.
Next row Work in patt to last 4dc, (2dc tog) twice. Turn. 120[122:126]dc.
Next row 1ch, (2dc tog) twice, work in patt to end. Turn. 118[120:124]dc.
Rep last 2 rows 3 times more. 106[108:112]dc.
Dec one st at armhole edge on next and every foll row 20[20:24] times in all. 86[88:88]dc.
Work one row without shaping. Dec one st at armhole edge on next and every foll alternate row 2[4:4] times in all, so ending at lower edge. 84dc.
Side shaping
Next row Work in patt over first 32dc. Turn, leaving rem sts unworked.
Work one row on these 32dc.
Next row Work in patt over first 28dc. Turn, leaving rem sts unworked.
Cont working 4dc less on every alternate row until there are 16dc. Fasten off.
With RS facing, miss 19 centre dc and rejoin yarn to next dc with a ss, 1ch, 1dc into same place as ss, work in patt to end. Turn.
Next row Work in patt over first 25dc. Turn, leaving rem sts unworked.
Work one row on these 25dc.
Next row Work in patt over first 17dc. Turn, leaving rem sts unworked.
Work one row on these 17dc.
Next row Work in patt over first 9dc. Fasten off.***

► **FRONT**
Work as for back from ** to **.
Neck shaping
Next row Miss first 9[9:10]dc and rejoin yarn to next dc with a ss, work in patt to end. Turn. 120[122:126]dc.
Dec one st at neck edge on next 2 rows. 118[120:124]dc.
Work one row without shaping.
Dec one st at neck edge on next row.
Rep last 2 rows twice more. 115[117:121]dc.
Work 25 rows without shaping.
Inc one st at neck edge on next and every foll alternate row 4 times in all. 119[121:125]dc.
Inc one st at neck edge on next row, so ending at neck edge. 120[122:126]dc.

Next row 10[10:11]ch, 1dc into 2nd ch from hook, 1dc into each of next 8[8:9]ch, work in patt to end. Turn. 129[131:136]dc.
Complete as for back from *** to ***.

▶ MAKING UP
Do not press. Join side seams. With RS facing and beg at right side seam, work dc evenly up right back armhole, along back neck easing in neck to correct width, down left back armhole, up left front armhole, along front neck easing in neck to correct width and down right front armhole, working 2dc into corners of straps. Join to first dc with a ss and fasten off. With RS facing, rejoin yarn with a ss to beg of back neck edge, 1ch, work 1dc around stem of each dc from the front along neck edge, turn, 1ch, work 1dc around stem of each dc from back along neck edge (see page 114). Fasten off.
Work a rolled edging in the same way along front neck edge.
Sew snap fasteners to ends of straps.

CHENILLE CHEQUERS

Chenille cotton in half treble filet net is worked here in overlapping blocks of colour. If you prefer not to crochet with bobbins, you could work a plain filet net in stripes or a solid colour. A simple double crochet rib is worked around the sleeves and lower edge and on the elegant wide collar.

▶ **SIZES**

To fit 81[86:91-96]cm/32[34:36-38]in bust.

Note: Figures for larger sizes are in square brackets. If there is only one set of figures, it applies to all sizes. *See diagram for finished measurements.*

▶ **MATERIALS**

See page 118 for further yarn information
Use a lightweight cotton chenille yarn (approx 145m per 50g):
250[250:300]g in A (brown)
100[100:150]g in B (rust)
100[150:200]g in C (steel grey)
3.50mm and 4.00mm crochet hooks *or size to obtain correct tension*

▶ **TENSION**

10 spaces and 13 rows to 10cm over filet colour patt using 3.50mm hook. *Check your tension before beginning.*

Note: When working filet colour patt do not carry colours across row, but use a separate bobbin of yarn for each square of colour (see page 112). When working from chart, read odd-numbered rows (RS) from right to left and even-numbered rows (WS) from left to right.

▶ **BACK**

Using smaller hook and A, make 97[105:113]ch.
Beg filet colour patt as foll:
Base row 1htr into 5th ch from hook, *1ch, miss 1ch, 1htr into next ch, rep from * to end. 47[51:55] spaces.
First size only:
1st row (RS) Using A, work 3ch *loosely*, miss first htr, 1htr into next htr, (1ch, 1htr into next htr) 5 times, *using B (1ch, 1htr into next htr) 9 times, using A (1ch, 1htr into next htr) 7 times*, rep from * to * once more, then using B (1ch, 1htr into next htr) 8 times, 1ch, 1htr into 2nd of 3ch. Turn. 47 spaces.
2nd row Using B, work 3ch *loosely*, miss first htr, 1htr into next htr, (1ch, 1htr into next htr) 7 times, *using A (1ch, 1htr into next htr) 7 times, using B (1ch, 1htr into next htr) 9 times*, rep from * to * once more, then using A (1ch, 1htr into next htr) 6 times, 1ch, 1htr into 2nd of 3ch. Turn.
3rd row Using A, work 3ch *loosely*,

miss first htr, 1htr into next htr, 1ch, 1htr into next htr, (1htr into next ch sp, 1htr into next htr) twice thus forming 2 blocks, (1ch, 1htr into next htr) twice, *using B (1ch, 1htr into next htr) 3 times, (1htr into next ch sp, 1htr into next htr) 4 times thus forming 4 blocks, (1ch, 1htr into next htr) twice, using A (1ch, 1htr into next htr) 3 times, (1htr into next ch sp, 1htr into next htr) twice thus forming 2 blocks, (1ch, 1htr into next htr) twice*, rep from * to * once more, then using B (1ch, 1htr into next htr) 3 times, (1htr into next ch sp, 1htr into next htr) 4 times, 1ch, 1htr into next htr, 1ch, 1htr into 2nd of 3ch. Turn.
2nd size only:
1st row (RS) Using B, work 3ch *loosely*, miss first htr, 1htr into first htr, *using A (1ch, 1htr into next htr) 7 times, using B (1ch, 1htr into next htr) 9 times*, rep from * to * twice more, then using A, 1ch, 1htr into next htr, 1ch, 1htr into 2nd of 3ch. Turn. 51 spaces.
2nd row Using A, work 3ch *loosely*, miss first htr, 1htr into next htr, *using B (1ch, 1htr into next htr) 9 times, using A (1ch, 1htr into next htr) 7 times*, rep from * to * twice more, then using B, 1ch, 1htr into next htr, 1ch, 1htr into 2nd of 3ch. Turn.
3rd row Using B, work 3ch *loosely*, miss first htr, 1htr into next htr, *using A (1ch, 1htr into next htr) 3 times, (1htr into next ch sp, 1htr into next htr) twice thus forming 2 blocks, (1ch, 1htr into next htr) twice, using B (1ch, 1htr into next htr) 3 times, (1htr into next ch sp, 1htr into next htr) 4 times thus forming 4 blocks, (1ch, 1htr into next htr) twice*, rep from * to * twice more, then using A, 1ch, 1htr into next htr, 1ch, 1htr into 2nd of 3ch. Turn.
3rd size:
1st row (RS) Using B, work 3ch *loosely*, miss first htr, 1htr into next htr, (1ch, 1htr into next htr) twice, rep from * to * of

first row for 2nd size 3 times in all, then using A (1ch, 1htr into next htr) 3 times, 1ch, 1htr into 2nd of 3ch. Turn. 55 spaces.
2nd row Using A, work 3ch *loosely*, miss first htr, 1htr into next htr, (1ch, 1htr into next htr) twice, rep from * to * of 2nd row for 2nd size 3 times in all, then using B (1ch, 1htr into next htr) 3 times, 1ch, 1htr into 2nd of 3ch. Turn.

3rd row Using B, work 3ch *loosely*, miss first htr, 1htr into next htr, (1ch, 1htr into next htr) twice, rep from * to * of 3rd row for 2nd size 3 times in all, then using A (1ch, 1htr into next htr) 3 times, 1ch, 1htr into 2nd of 3ch. Turn.
All sizes:
Cont in filet colour patt as set, foll chart and beg with 4th row of chart. When 30th chart row has been completed, beg with first row again. Work in patt, rep first-30th rows of chart, until back measures approx 54.5[55.5:56.5]cm from beg.
Neck shaping
Next row Work in patt across first 13[15:17] spaces, counting each block or space. Turn, leaving rem sts unworked.
Work one more row in patt on these sts. Fasten off.
Work 2nd side of neck in the same way.

▶ **FRONT**

Work as for back until front measures 45[46:47]cm from beg.
Neck shaping
Next row Work in patt across first 19[21:23] spaces, counting each block or space. Turn, leaving rem sts unworked.

Keeping patt correct, dec 2 spaces at beg of next row (by working ss over first 2 spaces), then dec one space at beg of every other row (neck edge) 4 times. 13[15:17] spaces.
Work without shaping until front measures same as back to shoulder. Fasten off.
Work 2nd side of neck in the same way, reversing shaping.

▶ **SLEEVES** (make 2)
Using smaller hook and A, make 69[73:77]ch. Work base row as for back. 33[35:37] spaces.
First size only:
1st row (RS) Using B, work 3ch *loosely*, miss first htr, 1htr into next htr, (1ch, 1htr into next htr) 7 times, using A (1ch, 1htr into next htr) 7 times, using B (1ch, 1htr into next htr) 9 times, using A (1ch, 1htr into next htr) 7 times, then using B, 1ch, 1htr into next htr, 1ch, 1htr into 2nd of 3ch. Turn. 33 spaces.
2nd size only:
1st row (RS) Using B, work 3ch *loosely*, miss first htr, 1htr into next htr, (1ch, 1htr into next htr) 8 times, using A (1ch, 1htr into next htr) 7 times, *using B (1ch, 1htr into next htr) 9 times, using A (1ch, 1htr into next htr) 7 times*, using B (1ch, 1htr into next htr) twice, 1ch, 1htr into 2nd of 3ch. Turn. 35 spaces.
3rd size only:
1st row (RS) Using A, work 3ch *loosely*, miss first htr, 1htr into next htr, rep from * to * of first row for 2nd size twice, then using B (1ch, 1htr into next htr) 3 times, 1ch, 1htr into 2nd of 3ch. Turn. 37 spaces.
All sizes:
Cont in filet colour patt as set, foll chart and beg with 2nd row of chart *and at*

the same time shape sides as foll:
Work 4 rows without shaping, inc one space at end of next 2 rows (by working 1htr, 1ch, 1htr into 2nd of 3ch at end of row). Rep from ** to ** 5 times more. 45[47:49] spaces.
Work in patt without shaping until sleeve measures 32cm from beg. Fasten off.

▶ **BACK RIB**
Using larger hook and A, make 9ch.
Base row 1dc into 2nd ch from hook, 1dc into each ch to end. Turn. 8dc.
1st row 1ch, working into *back* loops only, 1dc into each dc to end. Turn.
Rep last row to form rib patt. Cont in rib patt until rib fits across lower edge of back. Fasten off.

▶ **FRONT RIB**
Work as for back rib.

▶ **SLEEVE RIBS** (make 2)
Using smaller hook and A, work 1dc into each foundation chain across lower sleeve edge to slightly draw in width. Fasten off.
Work sleeve rib as for back rib until rib, slightly stretched, fits across lower sleeve edge. Fasten off.

▶ **COLLAR**
Join shoulder seams. Using smaller hook and A, work a round of dc evenly around neck edge and join with a ss to first dc. Fasten off.
Using larger hook and A, make 15ch and work base and first rows as for back rib. 14dc. Cont in rib patt until collar measures approx 92cm unstretched. Fasten off.

▶ **MAKING UP**
Do not press. Darn in all loose ends. Sew on back, front and sleeve ribs. Mark positions of sleeves 22[23:24]cm from shoulder seams. Sew on sleeves between markers. Join side and sleeve seams. Sew on collar, beg at centre front and easing in fullness at curves.

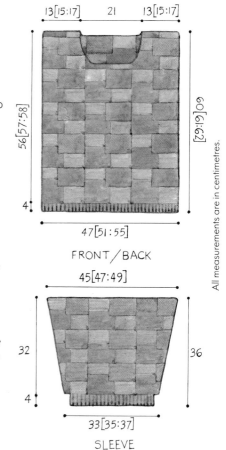

13[15:17] 21 13[15:17]
56[57:58] 60[61:62]
4
47[51:55]
FRONT / BACK

All measurements are in centimetres.

45[47:49]
32 36
4
33[35:37]
SLEEVE

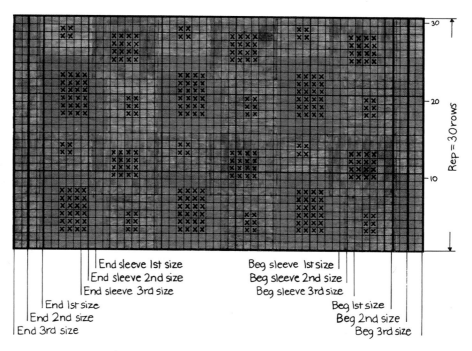

End sleeve 1st size
End sleeve 2nd size
End sleeve 3rd size
End 1st size
End 2nd size
End 3rd size

Beg sleeve 1st size
Beg sleeve 2nd size
Beg sleeve 3rd size
Beg 1st size
Beg 2nd size
Beg 3rd size

Rep = 30 rows

☐ one space   ☒ one block

APPENDIX

CROCHET TIPS

Here are some tips that even an experienced crocheter is well advised to read before beginning any of the sweaters in this book!

▶ WHAT SIZE TO MAKE?

After choosing the sweater you want to make, you must first decide which size to follow. Sizes are given according to bust measurement, but it is wise to consider a few factors before choosing to work the size which covers your bust measurement. The designer sizes garments according to the way a particular design should fit an 'average' shape. Most of us do not have a perfectly 'average' shape, however. For instance, if you know your shoulder width is narrow compared to your bust measurement, you may decide to work a smaller size than recommended — or vice versa. Likewise if your hip measurement is more than 10cm larger than your bust measurement, you may need a size larger than the recommended one. It's a good idea to measure the width of a similar sweater in your wardrobe and compare it to the one given on the measurement diagram provided.

▶ CHOOSING YARNS

Once you have chosen which size to crochet, you can purchase your yarn. It is wise to buy the yarn specified in the pattern instructions (see page 118). If this is not possible, choose a comparable yarn. Stick to the same type of yarn — substitute a smooth wool yarn for another smooth wool yarn, a mohair for a mohair, etc. Then compare the thickness of the substitute to the life-size photograph of the strand of yarn given on page 119. Calculate the total length of yarn you will need; the amount in metres is most important as the weight per metre varies drastically between different yarns due to their fibre content.

▶ CHECKING TENSION

Once you have your yarn, you are ready to begin. It can never be repeated enough to a crocheter — **check your tension before beginning.** If you can't achieve the correct tension with the hook size specified, you *must* change your hook size or your sweater will not come out to the correct size. Keep in mind that the hook size in the instructions is only a *guideline*. The frustration of working halfway up a back before realizing it is several centimetres wider or narrower than it should be is a common experience for many crocheters. Remember you will be *saving time if you take time to check your tension.*

Making a tension sample
Using the specified yarn, hook size and stitch pattern, work a piece which measures at least 15cm by 15cm. Lay the piece on a flat surface. In order not to stretch the fabric inadvertently do not smooth it into place but let it settle into its natural shape. With pins, mark out 10cm across the fabric. Then count the number of stitches between the pins. Do the same to count the number of rows. The side edges of the crochet fabric are usually less tight, so measure

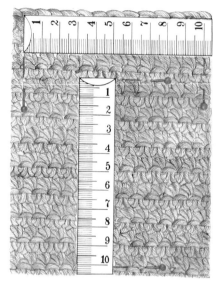

rows down the centre of the sample. Be sure to count half stitches and rows too.
* If you have too many stitches or rows per 10cm then make another sample with a larger hook.
* Too few stitches and rows per 10cm means a smaller hook is needed. *Keep testing until you are sure which hook size is best for you.* You will not regret the time spent.

▶ TOP TEN TIPS

Follow these important tips to improve your crochet tenfold!
● Always *check your tension* before beginning.
● Choose which size to make by comparing the diagram measurements to a similar sweater you have that *fits you comfortably.*
● When using a substitute yarn *buy one ball to start with* so that you can check its suitability first.
● Remember when substituting yarn to *match meterage and not weight* when deciding on amounts.
● *Measure your crochet pieces frequently* while crocheting to make sure your tension is not altering.
● *Recount stitches* after every few rows to avoid losing stitches.
● If the pattern instructions state *'at the same time',* read the whole sentence before proceeding.
● When measuring lengths *do not stretch the fabric* and *measure up the centre* of the piece.
● Use an *edge to edge seaming technique* whenever possible to avoid bulky seams.
● Keep a yarn label for pressing and washing requirements.

TEXTURE TECHNIQUES

There are many crochet techniques which create raised effects. The most obvious and pronounced are the various types of bobbles. Other more subtle textures are also shown here.

▶ WORKING AROUND STEMS

This technique is often used in combination with other types of stitches but it can also be used on its own to produce a textured surface much in the way that knit and purl

1

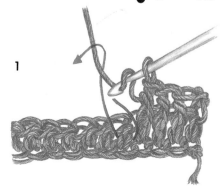

2

stitches are combined to form shapes in traditional Guernsey sweaters. An example of this method worked in half trebles is shown on the cotton design on page 64. Rolled edging and ribbing can also be made by working around the stem of double crochet and treble stitches respectively (see page 114).

▶ **SURFACE SLIP STITCH**

Surface slip stitch is formed in exactly the same way as chain stitch embroidery, but a crochet hook is used instead of a needle. It is a perfect way to add narrow vertical or horizontal stripes in a contrasting colour to plaids (as seen in the designs on pages 32 and 41). It is also sometimes used to make mock cables. The technique needs a little practice for the beginner but it is well worth the effort. Slip stitch crochet can be worked on any crochet ground, but when learning the technique start on a firm fabric such as double crochet.

1 When beginning at the lower edge of the crochet fabric, insert the hook from front to back through the foundation ch.

▶ **CHAIN STITCH EMBROIDERY**

This stitch is interchangeable with surface slip stitch. Although it is slower to work than the crochet technique, it is much easier. Unlike surface slip stitch it is not possible to work from a continuous strand of yarn, so begin by threading a blunt-ended needle with a strand of yarn aproximately 50cm long. For a thicker chain use two or three strands.

Fasten the yarn to the back of the work and bring the needle through to the front at the appropriate position. Reinsert the needle back through the hole where it was first brought through, then to the front again between the

▶ **BOBBLES**

There are several ways to make the round, raised textures called bobbles, puff stitches or popcorns. The technique that makes the most pronounced effect is shown here. This type of bobble with slight variations has been used on the designs on pages 54, 57 and 103. This bobble is worked on a half treble crochet ground and is made up of five stitches, but the bobble can easily be reduced or enlarged by decreasing or increasing the size of stitches or the number of stitches.

Work to the position of the bobble and then work 1htr, 3tr, 1htr all into the next stitch. Remove the hook from the loop, drawing the loop out slightly so that it will not unravel. Reinsert the

1 Make a base row of htr. Make 2ch to count as the first htr. To work around the stem from the front of the work, yrh and insert the hook from front to back between the first and 2nd stitches, then behind the 2nd stitch and back to the front between the 2nd and 3rd stitches. Complete htr as usual.

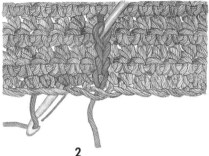

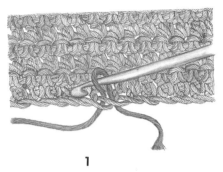

1

Then holding the yarn at the back of the work throughout, yrh and draw a loop through to the front. Leave a loose end long enough (approximately 10cm) to darn in on the wrong side later. Remember to work loosely as you proceed so that the fabric does not pull together.

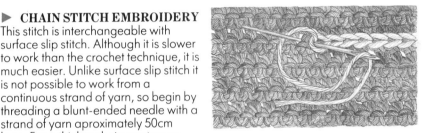

next two stitches (or rows), keeping the loop of yarn at the front under the point of the needle. Continue in this way inserting the needle to the back through the previous hole and to the front again a between the next two stitches.

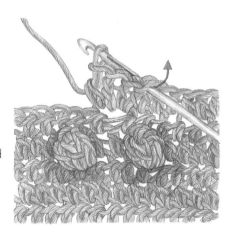

hook into the top of the first htr of the group of five stitches. Then draw the working loop through and continue in htr until the next bobble is reached.

2 To work around the stem from the back of the work, yrh and insert the hook from back to front between the stitch being worked and the previous stitch, then in front of the stitch and to the back between the next two stitches. Complete the htr in the usual way.

2

2 Keeping the loop on the hook, insert the hook between the first two rows. Yrh and draw a loop through the fabric and the loop on the hook. Continue in this way always inserting the hook between the following two rows. For a horizontal stripe work between the stitches instead of the rows.

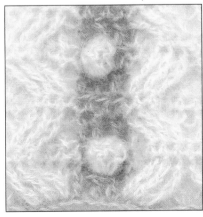

This detail from the jacket on page 32 shows the white stripes which can be worked in slip stitch or chain stitch.

Bobbles are worked between the cables on the slipover on page 54. Work bobbles and cables in two colours to emphasize the texture.

COLOUR PATTERNS

Crochet is at its most exciting when the basic stitches are worked in a contrast of stunning colours and beautiful fibres. The basic colour pattern tehniques shown here are so simple to grasp that they are within reach of the most inexperienced crocheter.

▶ **CHANGING COLOURS**

The most versatile method of working crochet colour patterns is called 'colourwork'. Each colour is used for as many stitches as indicated in the instructions or on the chart. Successful results in colourwork crochet are dependent upon knowing the correct method for changing from one colour to another in a row.

The pattern chosen here to illustrate colour changes is a simple check. When working with only two colours in a row, the colour not in use can either be carried along the top of the row below and worked over or stranded loosely across the back of the work.

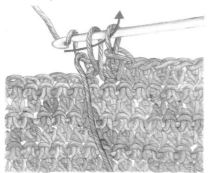

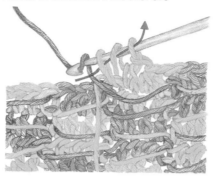

Double crochet

When the design being worked is in dc, work to the last stitch in the first colour. Insert the hook into the next stitch, yrh and draw a loop through. Drop the first colour and using the second colour, yrh and draw a loop through. Always change to the new colour in this way — by working the last yrh of the previous stitch in the new colour.

Half treble

Change colours on htr in the same way as for dc by working the last yrh of the previous stitch in the new colour, so that the stitch before the new colour starts is 'closed' by the new colour. The work is shown here on the wrong side and the yarn not in use is being stranded across the back of the fabric. Always drop the colour not in use to the wrong side of the work.

Treble

For treble colourwork, the new colour is also used to close the previous stitch before beginning the new colour. When the colour not in use is carried across the top of the previous row and worked over as shown here, the crochet fabric is reversible. Do not pull the new colour too tight when picking it up to use again or your work will become too narrow.

▶ **BLOCKS OF COLOUR**

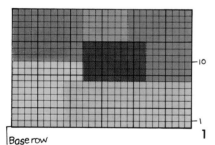

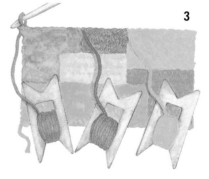

Any number of colour designs can be charted on graph paper and then translated into crochet. When there are only two colours used in each row and both colours are used alternately across the row, they can both be carried across the row. But if isolated motifs or large blocks of several colours are being worked, then separate balls or bobbins of each colour are needed. In this way each section uses its own separate source of yarn which is picked up and used when that section is reached. Plastic bobbins are worthwhile purchases as you can control the flow of yarn from them and avoid tangled balls.

1 Wind a long length of each colour onto a bobbin. Work the crochet following the chart square by square.

Odd-numbered rows (RS) are read from right to left and even-numbered rows (WS) from left to right.

2 When changing colours drop the first colour to the wrong side of the work, and work the last yrh of the previous stitch with the new colour.

3 The bobbins hang at the back of the work and the yarn is unwound as it is used. If you do not want to darn in loose ends when the piece is completed, work over the ends when stopping and starting a new block of colour.

This is a detail from Colour Blocks on page 83. The colour pattern on the slipover is worked using a separate bobbin of yarn for each colour.

▶ WEAVING CROCHET

Some colour pattern techniques involve the combination of different basic crochet stitches. Colourful plaids and tweeds, for example, can be made by weaving onto a ground of filet crochet net (see page 48).

To weave onto a striped htr filet net, take three or four strands of yarn threaded through a blunt-ended needle. The strands should be long enough to work the number of vertical rows to be woven in that colour plus approximately 30cm extra for adjusting and darning in. Beginning at the lower right-hand edge of the piece, pass the needle through the foundation ch under the first ch space, leaving a 15cm loose end at the beginning. Then weave *loosely* in and out of the spaces towards the top of the fabric.

At the top of the fabric pass the needle through the ch above the last ch space. Then insert the needle through the ch above the next ch space to the left. Weave down the fabric working *over* the rows worked *under* in the last vertical stripe and vice versa. When the vertical stripes in the first colour are complete, continue with the next colour and so on. After weaving the entire piece, loosen and smooth out the woven strands, matching the measurements of the piece to the garment diagram. Darn in the loose ends.

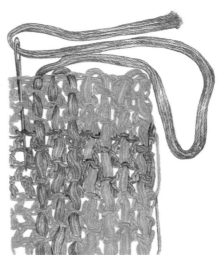

▶ ELONGATED STITCHES

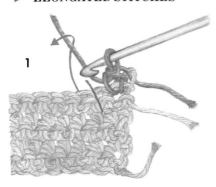

A very easy way to make colour patterns or isolated motifs is with elongated double crochet. The stitches form long V shapes on the front and the back of the crochet fabric and are especially effective when worked in a yarn which contrasts in texture with the background. Many shapes can be formed with the elongated stitches and instructions for a triangle shape are given here.

1 This is worked onto a base of several rows of dc. At the beginning of the pattern row change to the new colour or different textured yarn and work 1ch and 1dc into the first stitch. Insert the hook from the front to the back through the top of the stitch one row below the next stitch and yrh.

2 Draw a loop through the fabric extending it up as high as the previous stitch and working *loosely* so that the background is not pulled together. Complete the dc in the usual way.

3 Work an elongated dc into the top of the stitch two rows below the next stitch, then one three rows below the next stitch and four rows below the next stitch. Continue working in this way, counting stitches carefully across the previous row.

CROCHET EDGINGS

Remember that the success of a crochet garment depends on its neat, even edgings. There is no sense in making beautiful crochet pieces and topping them off with careless finishes. Take your time with edgings and you will have a garment to be proud of.

▶ DOUBLE CROCHET EDGING

The simplest and most common crochet edging is the double crochet edging. Instructions usually call for double crochet to be worked 'evenly along the edge'. Unfortunately there is no steadfast rule that will determine exactly how many stitches to work along an edge, so the only answer is to experiment until a smooth finish is achieved. If too few stitches are worked, the edge will pull together and if too many are worked, the edge will curl. Keep trying until you get it right. It helps to lay the work flat as you go to check for tightness.

1 Join the yarn to the fabric with a ss, inserting the hook through the edge of the fabric, yrh and draw a loop through. Work 1ch and then a dc into the same place as the ss was worked. Continue along the edge in dc.

2 For a firmer finish work a round of ss *loosely* over the first round of dc. Work each ss by inserting the hook under *both* loops at the top of each dc, yrh and draw a loop through the dc and the loop on the hook.

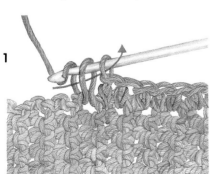

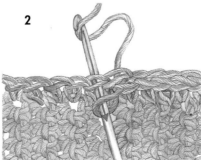

113

► ROLLED EDGING

This interesting edging gives a very attractive finish to your crochet garment. It has more body than a simple double crochet edging and is made by working double crochet around the stems of the stitches in the previous row. Shown here worked in rows, the rolled edging can also be worked in *rounds* in which case the right side would always be facing and the stitches would be worked around the stem from the *front* in every round. The number of rows or rounds worked depends on how wide the edging is to be. Two rounds are sufficient to form an edging which will roll to the right side of the fabric and cover the base row.

1 Begin with a row of dc along the right side of the fabric. If you are working in rows, turn the work at the end of the row. Work 1ch and 1dc into the first

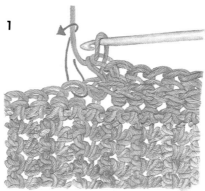

stitch. Insert the hook from back to front into the space before the next stitch, around the next stitch and from front to back through the next space. Draw a loop through and complete the dc in the usual way. Continue working a dc around the stem of each stitch from the back to the end of the row, working 1dc into the last stitch. Turn the work so that the right side is facing again.

2 Work 1ch and 1dc into the first stitch. Insert the hook from front to back into the space before the next stitch, around the next stitch and from back to front through the next space. Draw a loop through and complete the dc in the usual way. Continue working a dc around the stem of each stitch from the front to the end, working 1dc into the last stitch. Fasten off. For a deeper edge, increase the number of rows.

► DOUBLE CROCHET RIB

Crochet rib is ideal for a wider edging. The double crochet rib was developed to imitate knitted ribbing and although it is not nearly as elastic as the knitted version it is as close an approximation as is possible with crochet. Often the rib is worked in a strip and turned sideways to form the base for the first row of the back, front or sleeves. Generally it is better to add this ribbing after the garment pieces are completed; you can then adjust the length of the ribbing.

1 Work the base row in dc to the width required for the depth of the ribbing. *Turn and work 1ch. Inserting the hook into the *back* loop only at the top of each stitch, work in dc to the end of the row. Repeat from * to form the ribbing, working the edge stitches tightly.

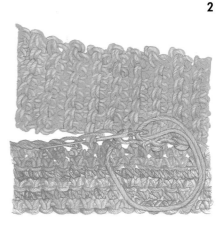

2 When the ribbing is the required length, fasten off. With the right side facing, sew the ribbing to the edge of the crochet fabric with a simple running stitch. If the ribbing is being added to

the side edge of the crochet piece, work a dc edging onto the garment selvedge first. Always place the garment edge over the ribbing while seaming.

► TREBLE RIBBING

The treble ribbing is not as elastic as the double crochet ribbing, but it produces raised horizontal 'ribs' similar in appearance to knitted ribs. As the effect is purely decorative this technique should not be used where a snug or stretchy fabric is required. The relief texture is achieved by working treble stitches around the stems of the stitches of the previous row (see page 110). For treble ribbing at the base of the back, front or sleeves, work the ribbing to the required depth and then begin the main stitch pattern. For neck or armhole ribbing work the base row of treble directly onto the crochet fabric.

1 To begin, work a base row in tr. Turn and make 3ch to count as the first

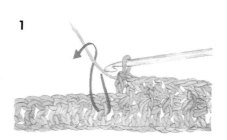

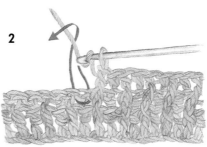

stitch. Miss the first stitch in the row below, yrh and insert the hook *from the front* around the next stitch. Complete the tr in the usual way. Work the next stitch around the tr *from the back*. Continue working one stitch around the stem from the front and from the back alternately. Work 1htr into the 3rd ch at the end.

2 Work the next row in the same way as the last row but working around the stem from the back on stitches that were worked around the stem from the front in the last row and vice versa. In this way the horizontal 'ribs' are formed.

KNITTED EDGINGS

For any crocheter with basic knitting skills, knitted edgings offer an effective alternative to crochet edgings. Knitting will provide a softer and more flexible finished edge to the firmer and crisper crochet fabric.

▶ PICKING UP STITCHES

Before a knitted edging can be worked, stitches must be picked up along the edge of the crochet fabric. Stitches are either picked up along the foundation chain, the last row of stitches or along the row ends. The number of stitches to be picked up will be given in the instructions. These stitches should be dispersed *evenly* along the edge specified. One way to ensure that the stitches are picked up evenly is to divide the edge being worked into tenths, mark them with pins and then work one tenth of the stitches required across each section. With the right side facing insert the point of the knitting needle through the edge of the fabric and wind the yarn around the needle. Draw the yarn through. The first loop is now on the

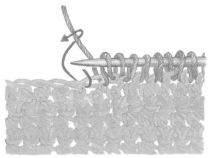

knitting needle. Continue along the edge of the fabric in the same way drawing through loops until there are the required number of stitches on the needle. Check that the stitches have been picked up evenly and redo if necessary.

▶ ROLLED EDGING

1

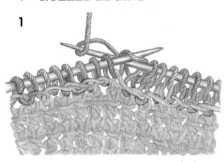

This edging forms a neat, rounded edge similar to a bold piping. It is an effective border for armholes, necklines and cuffs. Unlike crochet rolled edging, the knitted version is worked so that it rolls to the wrong side of the fabric instead of to the right side. It is worked in reverse stocking stitch so that the first row is a knit row, the second row a purl row and so on until the edging is the required depth. The edging can be worked in rows or in rounds with a circular knitting needle. When worked in rounds, every row is purled and the right side is always facing. Pick up the required number of stitches along the edge of the fabric and hold the knitting needle with the loops in the left hand and the empty needle in the right hand ready to begin the first row of edging.

2

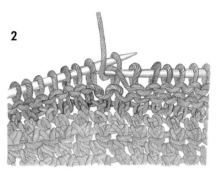

1 The edging here is worked in rows. To knit the first row, insert the right-hand needle from front to back through the front of the first loop. Wind the yarn around the tip of the right-hand needle, draw the yarn through the loop to form a new loop on the right-hand needle, dropping the loop just worked through from the left-hand needle. Continue working knit stitches one at a time in this way to the end of the row.

2 Turn the work so that the right side is facing. To purl the 2nd row, insert the right-hand needle from right to left through the front of the first loop. Wind the yarn around the tip of the right-hand needle and draw the yarn through the loop to form a new loop, dropping the loop just worked through

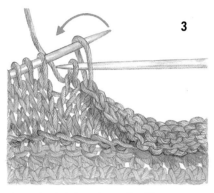

3

from the left-hand needle. Continue working purl stitches in this way to the end of the row.

3 Work one more knit row followed by one more purl row. On the next row knit the first two stitches. Using the left-hand needle, pass the first stitch over the second and off the needle to cast off the first stitch. Knit the next stitch and cast off another stitch. Continue in this way to the end. When one stitch remains break off the yarn, leaving a long enough piece to darn in later. Draw the end through the loop to fasten off. The edging will roll to the wrong side of the fabric. There is no need to stitch the edging down to the wrong side. If it is not rolling firmly, unravel the cast off row and cast off again more tightly.

▶ RIBBING

Knitted ribbing is more flexible and elastic than crochet ribbing. Begin the ribbing by picking up stitches along the edge of the crochet fabric. When picking up along a neckline, armhole or any rounded edge, pick up fewer stitches along the curved sections than along the straight sections so that the finished ribbing will lie flat around the curves.

1 On the first row knit one stitch and purl one stitch alternately to the end of the row. This creates an elastic rib called 'K1, P1 rib'.

1

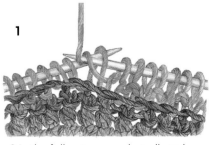

2 In the following rows knit all stitches purled in the last row and vice versa. Continue until the ribbing is the correct depth then *cast off in rib* by knitting and purling stitches in the same way while casting off.

2

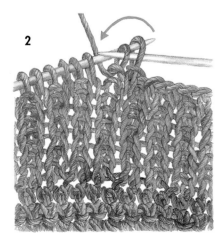

TUNISIAN CROCHET

Tunisian crochet is a cross between knitting and crochet and may have been the precursor to knitting. This kinship is most evident in Tunisian crochet 'knit' stitch.

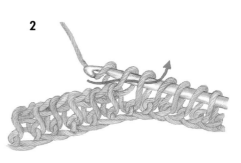

▶ PLAIN STITCH

Tunisian crochet is worked with a long hook with a knob on the end. The fabric is made by picking up loops all along the work, casting them off in the following row, then picking up loops again and so on. Because of the way all the loops must fit onto the hook the width of the fabric is limited by the length of the hook and the number of loops it can hold.

1 To work the basic stitch (plain stitch), begin with a foundation ch. Insert the hook into the second loop from the hook, yrh and draw a loop through the ch. Continue in this way drawing up a loop through each ch to the end. Do not turn but work all rows with the right side facing.

2 For the next row (the return row — right side facing) yrh and draw a loop through the first loop on the hook. *Yrh and draw a loop through the next two loops on the hook. Repeat from * until there is one loop left on the hook. This loop forms the first stitch of the next row.

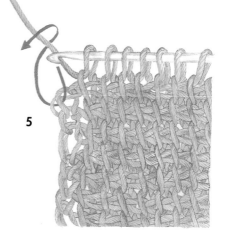

3 Miss the first vertical loop in the row below and insert the hook from right to left through the next vertical loop. Yrh and draw a loop through. There are now two loops on the hook.

4 Continue in this way from right to left across the row. This row is called a

loop row. Each loop row is followed by a return row.

5 At the end of each loop row be sure to insert the hook through the centre of the last loop at the edge so that there are two vertical strands of yarn at the extreme left-hand edge.

▶ KNIT STITCH

The return row of chain stitches is the only thing that separates Tunisian knit stitch from knitting. Although the resulting Tunisian fabric is thicker and less elastic than stocking stitch, it still has an attractive feel and texture if worked on a large enough hook. After a knit stitch piece has been completed it should be pressed with a warm iron and a damp cloth, so be sure to use a yarn that can be pressed.

1 Work the foundation ch and the first loop row and return row as for plain stitch. Then begin the next row by missing the first vertical loop below and inserting the hook from front to back through the centre of the next vertical loop. The hook should pass through the loop *under* the ch formed by the return row. Yrh and draw a loop through.

2 Continue to the end of the row drawing a loop through each vertical loop in the same way. Work return and loop rows alternately to form the fabric. The last loop stitch of each loop row should be worked exactly as for plain stitch.

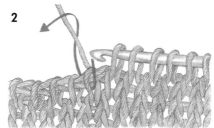

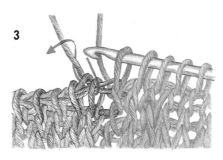

3 When working colour patterns in knit stitch, change to the new colour on a loop row where indicated in the instructions, dropping the first colour to the back of the work. Use separate lengths of yarn if each colour is used only in one area. If the colours alternate across the row, strand the colour not in use *loosely* across the back of the work.

4 When working return rows on a colour pattern, draw the matching colour through each loop, changing colours when the first loop in a new colour is reached. If the colours are used alternately across the row, strand the colour not in use across the back as for loop rows. To avoid long, loose strands, work over and under them on the following row.

MAKING UP

Painstaking execution of blocking and seaming will add professional polish to your crochet. If you put as much thought and patience into these finishing touches as you have into your crocheting, you will be well rewarded.

▶ BLOCKING AND PRESSING

Hesitate before applying an iron to your crochet pieces! First read the pattern instructions and the yarn label for advice. Some yarns will not react well to heat and will begin to melt down if mistreated, so heed the yarn label when it says *do not press* or shows the international symbol of a crossed-out iron. An iron with dots on it means that ironing won't damage the yarn: one dot means a cool iron should be used, two dots indicates a warm iron, and three dots a hot iron. Highly textured crochet fabrics should not be flattened by ironing. If you want to block your pieces into shape but they will not stand pressing, you can always wet block. This is done by pinning the pieces out on a padded surface and covering them with a damp towel. Leave to dry, then unpin. If pressing is indicated in your instructions and permitted on the yarn label, it is still important to treat your crochet fabric gently. Pin the pieces out with the right side facing down. Cover them with a damp (or dry cloth as directed) and press separately, lifting the iron and not dragging it when you move it across the piece.

▶ EDGE TO EDGE SEAM

This type of seam produces a flat, invisible join. It is sometimes called overcasting. Use it wherever possible to avoid bulky seams. Thread a blunt-ended needle with a length of yarn. Then place the crochet pieces together with the right sides facing and line up the rows. Take special care when lining up stripes and plaids. Pin together at intervals if desired.

Work the seam by inserting the needle under one strand of yarn on one side and across to the other side.

▶ BACKSTITCH SEAM

This is sometimes necessary where the edge of the crochet piece has 'stepped' increases or decreases. Work small, even backstitches as close to the edge as possible. Before beginning, secure the yarn to the edge of the fabric with a few short overcast stitches. Never use knots as they will unravel with wear. Work each stitch by reinserting the needle back through the fabric at the same place it emerged from the previous stitch and passing it through to the front a short distance away.

▶ SLIP STITCH SEAM

This is the quickest seaming method. Use a hook one or two sizes smaller than the hook used for the crochet fabric and work each stitch loosely. Double crochet stitch can also be used for a seam. It is more elastic but creates a bulkier edge. Insert the hook through both thicknesses and draw a loop through. *Insert the hook through again and draw a loop through the fabric and the loop on hook. Repeat from * until the length of seam is joined.

▶ CROCHET SYMBOLS

Crochet stitch patterns can be written in a shorthand of international symbols. Each type of stitch is represented by a symbol which resembles the shape or height of the stitch itself. There are numerous symbols for various types and combinations of stitches but only the basic stitch symbols have been used in this book and are given below.

- ⊙ first chain
- ◯ chain
- ✛ double crochet
- ⊤ half treble
- ⟊ treble
- ⟊⟋ double treble

YARNS

These are life-size photographs of the yarns used for each of the sweaters in the book. The labels which describe the thicknesses of the yarns as *fine*, *lightweight* and *medium weight* are only meant as a general guideline. The brand names are those of the yarns used by the designer in crocheting the sweaters for this book. For best results, use these brands. If you are attempting to find a substitute, place the yarn next to the photograph to check that it is the same thickness. Always choose the same type of yarn as a substitute — i.e. choose another mohair for a mohair, a slub yarn for a slub yarn, a smooth yarn for a smooth yarn, etc. For information on how to calculate quantities when substituting a different yarn, see page 110.

Note: Fibre content is given in parentheses after each yarn name. The colours given in the instructions are purely descriptive and are meant to serve as a guide; they are not the same colour names used by the yarn manufacturer.

page 12 Broad stripes
medium weight acrylic and rayon yarn — the specific brand used for this sweater has been discontinued

page 15 Stripe panels
fine wool tweed yarn — Rowan *Light Tweed* (wool)

page 18 Checked stripes
lightweight mohair — Pingouin *Mohair 50* (mohair/acrylic/wool)

page 22 Stripes on stripes
lightweight wool yarn — Rowan *Lightweight DK* (wool)

page 26 Stripes & squares
lightweight cotton yarn — MC and D = Rowan *Cabled Mercerised Cotton* (cotton)
lightweight metallic yarn — A, B and C = Pingouin *Place Vendome* (viscose/polyester)

page 32 Bold block plaid
lightweight wool yarn — G = Anny Blatt *No 4* (wool)
lightweight mohair — A, B, C, D, E and F = Anny Blatt *Soft Anny* (kid mohair/polycholorid)

page 36 Tricolour check
lightweight cotton yarn — Rowan *Cabled Mercerised Cotton* (cotton)

page 38 Textured checks
lightweight wool yarn — A, C, D, F, G and H = Rowan *Lightweight DK* (wool)
lightweight cotton knop yarn — B and E = Scheepjeswol *Miranda* (cotton/acrylic)

page 41 Check & plaid
lightweight cotton yarn — F and G = Rowan *Cabled Mercerised Cotton* (cotton)
fine wool tweed yarn — A, B, C, D and E = Rowan *Light Tweed* (wool)

page 44 Buffalo plaid
fine wool tweed yarn — Rowan *Light Tweed* (wool)

page 48 Woven plaid
lightweight cotton chenille — Rowan *Fine Cotton Chenille* (cotton/polyester)

page 54 Cables
lightweight mohair — Anny Blatt *Soft Anny* (kid mohair/polycholorid)

page 57 Zigzags
fine slubbed cotton and linen yarn — Scheepjeswol *Linnen* (cotton/linen)

page 60 Clusters
lightweight wool and silk yarn — Baruffa/Lane Borgosesia *Serilana* (wool/silk)

page 64 Basketweave
lightweight cotton yarn — Rowan *Cabled Mercerised Cotton* (cotton)

page 72 Fans
medium weight wool yarn — B = Rowan *Designer DK Wool* (wool)
lightweight cotton and viscose yarn — A
lightweight cotton chenille — MC = Rowan *Fine Cotton Chenille* (cotton/polyester)

page 76 Leaves
medium weight slubbed cotton yarn — Scheepjeswol *Granada* (cotton)

page 80 Diamonds
lightweight cotton yarn — Rowan *Cabled Mercerised Cotton* (cotton)

page 83 Colour blocks
lightweight wool yarn — A, B, C, D, E, F, G, H and I = Rowan *Lightweight DK* (wool)
lightweight mohair — J = lightweight mohair, nylon and acrylic yarn

page 86 Winter flowers
lightweight wool yarn — Rowan *Lightweight DK* (wool)

page 90 Bobbled Fair Isle
lightweight cotton yarn — E = Pingouin *Fil D'Ecosse No 5* (cotton)
F, G and H = Rowan *Cabled Mercerised Cotton* (cotton)
lightweight wool yarn — A, B, C and D = Pingouin *Pingofine* (acrylic/wool)

page 94 Waves & checks
medium weight slubbed cotton yarn — Scheepjeswol *Granada* (cotton)

page 100 Scalloped lace
lightweight mohair and silk — Pingouin *Mohair et Soie* (kid mohair/silk)

page 103 Bobbled lace
lightweight cotton yarn — Rowan *Cabled Mercerised Cotton* (cotton)

page 106 Chenille chequers
lightweight cotton chenille — Rowan *Fine Cotton Chenille* (cotton/polyester)

page 12

page 15

page 18

page 22

page 26

page 32

page 36

page 38

page 41

page 44

page 48

page 54

page 57

page 60

page 64

page 72

page 76

page 80

page 83

page 86

page 90

page 94

page 100

page 103

page 106

YARN SUPPLIERS

For information about yarn availability, mail order and retail shops, contact the yarn manufacturers.

ANNY BLATT
UK:
Laines Anny Blatt (UK) Ltd
Bull Bridge
Ambergate, Derby DE5 2EY
Tel: 077385-6025

USA:
Anny Blatt
24770 Crestview Court
Farmington Hills, MI 48018

CANADA:
Anny Blatt
Diamond Yarns Inc
9697 St. Laurence Blvd
Montreal, Quebec H3L 2N1

AUSTRALIA:
Anny Blatt AUST Pty Ltd
26 Punch Sreet
Artarmon, NSW 2064
Tel: (02) 439 4266

BARUFFA/LANE BORGOSESIA
UK:
Serilana available from Maxwell Cartlidge
Ltd

USA:
Baruffa/Lane Borgosesia
RD2, Fields Lane
N. Salem, NY 10560

MAXWELL CARTLIDGE LTD
UK (only):
P.O. Box 33
Colchester
Essex

PINGOUIN
UK:
Pingouin
7-11 Lexington St
London W1R 4BU
Tel: 01-439 8891

USA:
V. Hoover Promafil Corp
PO Box 100
Jamestown, SC 29453

CANADA:
Pingouin
Promafil Canada Ltée
1500 Jules Poitras
St. Laurent, PQ H4N 1X7

AUSTRALIA:
Pingouin Aust Pty Ltd
4757 Collins Sreet
Alexandria NSW 2015

ROWAN
UK:
Rowan Yarns
Green Lane Mill
Washpit, Holmfirth
Huddersfield HD7 1RW
West Yorkshire
Tel: 0484-686714

USA:
Rowan Yarns
Westminster Trading
5 Northern Boulevard
Amherst NH 03031
Tel: (603) 886 5041

AUSTRALIA:
Sunspun Enterprises Pty
195 Canterbury Road
Canterbury
Vic 3126

NEW ZEALAND:
Creative Fashion Centre
PO Box 45083
Epuni Railway
Lower Hutt

SCHEEPJESWOL
UK:
Scheepjeswol
PO Box 48
No 7 Colemeadow Road
Redditch B98 9NZ
Tel: 0527-61056

USA:
Scheepjeswol USA
155 Lafayette Ave
N. White Plains, NY 10603

CANADA:
Scheepjeswol (Canada) Ltd
400 Blvd Montée de Liesse
Montreal, Quebec H4T 1N8

NEW ZEALAND/AUSTRALIA:
Thorobred Scheepjeswol Ltd
300 Richmond Road
Grey Lynn, PO Box 52028
Kingsland, Auckland

ACKNOWLEDGMENTS

The author would like to thank Anne Farmer (Cambridgeshire Knitters) and her crocheters for their help in producing many sweaters for the book. She also thanks her mother Jean Myers Miller for introducing her to the joy of textiles and for making three of the sweaters with her usual needlework excellence.
The publishers would like to thank the following people for their help and advice in the production of this book; Suzi Read for checking the patterns; Barbara Jones (Artistic Licence) for hair and make-up; Sarah Gisborne (Models One-Plus) and Vanessa Spiro (Bookings) for the modelling; Fanny Rush for the styling for fashion photography; and *Accessorize* for all jewellery.

Editor Charyn Jones
Art Editor Louise Tucker

General Editor Pippa Rubinstein

Managing Editor Susan Berry
Art Director Debbie MacKinnon

Fashion Photography Julie Fisher
Still-life Photography Chris Crofton, Assistant Jayne Pearce

Step-by-step Illustration Lindsay Blow
Fashion Illustration Colin Barnes
Charts and measurement diagrams David Ashby